A Historical Account of Student Movement in Bengal

Colonial and Post-Colonial Experiences (1828-1977)

A Historical Account of Student Movement in Bengal

Colonial and Post-Colonial Experiences (1828-1977)

Dr. Swapan Kumar Pain

Delta Book World
New Delhi-110 002

ISBN: 978-93-85719-26-4
First Published in 2021

Published by **Abhishek Goel** on behalf of

Delta Book World
G-4, Prahlad House
4832/24, Ansari Road
New Delhi - 110 002 (India)

Tel.: 011-4707 2321
E-mail: deltabookworld@gmail.com
Website: www.kaveribooks.com

PRINTED IN INDIA

Dedicated to

My Father

Late Adhir Kumar Pain

Foreword

The present study throws light on the activities of the students and their participation in the socio-economic issues of Bengal since Derozian movement to 1977. After the establishment of Colonial Rule, the educated elite at first welcomed them, but soon they became skeptic, and they demanded freedom of speech, freedom of association, and more employment opportunities for the Indians, which attracted the youth's minds and students. There were innumerable protests among the Bengali students against British imperialism. For example, protest against Macaulay's Report, Young Bengal Movement, protest against Ilbert Bill, Partition of Bengal, Carlyle Circular and participation in Gandhian Movements.

After Independence, West Bengal had to face a series of problems as a newly born state i.e. political instability, growing economic gloom, problem of immigration and migration, food crisis, Naxalite movement, Indo-Chinese, Indo-Pak and Bangladesh Liberation War, unemployment etc. created an untoward situation throughout West Bengal. During this period, the spontaneous popular protests were drawing the attention of students of Bengal and they involved themselves in those movements for the sake of nation building process. This work has full of information in connection with social, economic, political, cultural and humanistic movements of students in different parts of West Bengal.

The global student movements have been one of the most dramatic and noble social phenomenon of the 1960s throughout the world. To understand totally about the evolution of the student movement of Bengal, Dr. Pain mentions some ideas about the international socio-political perspective and the continuous student uprising of the then world at large. Whatever those student movements were fully in right way or, in wrong, rather it was more important to judge these movements in the light of national and international causation or incidents. It was established that in one hand, the main cause of the student movements during the 1960s and 1970s was the socio-economic crisis of the country, on the other hand, there were so many living examples to draw inspiration from the movements of the students of France and Germany against capitalism, uncompromised students' movements of Europe and America, the Vietnamese Liberation Movement against American imperialism, the cultural movements of Communist China etc. These created an adverse reaction in the minds of the Bengali students from which faith of the entire student organizations upon existing system was shattered down into pieces. In addition to that the students also came to know about the facts of suffered and poverty-stricken people of the Third World which intensified the momentum of this movement. This disparity in the socio-economic fabric of the society of the two different continents leads to a depression among the students. On the other hand, the conscious students group raised vehement protest against the existing ruling set up, which was also reflected among the students of West Bengal as well as throughout India. The contemporary global students' movement and the various issues left a vibrant impact upon student community of West Bengal at large.

The participation of the students in the popular movements of West Bengal was one of the remarkable episodes of history. After the achievement of Independence, the students involved in various socio-economic movements, such as the movement against the brutal murder of Gandhiji, movement in favour of the refugees, movement against the hike of Tram fare, Teachers' movement, and Anti-Merger movement of West Bengal & Bihar and so on. During this period most of the student movement had taken place against the unpopular activities of the Independent Government, but in favour of socio-economic development of the country. The goals of the different movements of the students, fighting under different political banners are not only political, but also social, economic, humanistic and cultural.

During the period of economic crisis (1959-1966) of Bengal, the students played an important role. At this time the embryo of the students' disaffection matured into a decisive shape. The main reasons were the internal political and social ferment and very shocking economic crisis. Before the outset of the 1960s, the historic Food Movement in Calcutta along with the whole state of West Bengal shocked the people of Bengal. This Food Movement took a serious turn in 1959 and 1966. It was one of the most significant instances of mass movements in West Bengal. The failure of the government to secure and distribute food grains together with the increasing population pressure after partition led to massive hoarding and black marketing which synthetically increased the food price. The opposition leaders of Bengal took a twine policy in this regard. They brought the issue of food paucity inside the State Assembly and thereby, drew public and media attention. Secondly, as a tactic of organizing anti-government mass movements, they formed various issue-based committees like the *Price Increase and Famine Resistance Committee (PIFRC)* for broader public support. In this historic movement the revolutionary role of the students became obvious with their involvement to the movement.

The outbreak of an agrarian movement at *Naxalbari* was an event of great significance not only in the history of the agrarian movements but also in the subsequent movements also.

One significant feature of the movement was the participation of students in the movement at par with peasants. During this time the student movement broke away from the vestige of its past and took a new line of operation. Statistically in the student and youth movements, the active participation of the students and youths was to the turn of twenty to twenty five percent. But this movement could be as powerful as many others provided it with unquestioning support. A reference has been made to the explosion of anger of students but that was a mixture of socio-economic and political reactions. How far student community was conscious about the social realities? It can be ascertained by dividing it into three parts. First of these three parts is the political consciousness and this part is very well organized and usually led the students' demonstration. To the second part belonged a group of active workers who usually works keeping the leadership at the centre. Some of these workers were conscious, some less conscious and still others were there who usually took part in different students' movements on account of either on the ground of humanity or democracy. In almost all the students' organizations these democrats and humanists were usually account for large number. The third part of the student community was a mammoth crowd of students who never supported any organization but jumped into action whenever these movements gained maximum momentum. In the first half of the year 1971 after the Bangladesh Liberation War, a vacuum in the political scene of West Bengal became conspicuous because of the backing out of the radical students from the path of democratic movement. The said vacuum was inevitably filled up by the SFI and Chhatra Parishad, ostensibly the self-seekers. This makes it clear that the terrorist activities of the radical students could not get any favourable support from the society. Therefore, it is true that the students being stimulated by the Naxalbari flare up could realize the importance of the necessity of attending to the problems of the peasants. They repeatedly proposed to occupy the position of power through armed struggle. But their idea about the problems of the peasants and the armed struggle for removing them was not clear. The character of the movements of the students of West Bengal began changing since 1960s. Starting as nationalists they gradually assumed left and extreme ideology. In place of the mass student organizations, a number of local groups mostly of an informal nature have developed.

The student movement had left a deep impact in a number of ways. The patriotism, sacrifice and courage of the students earned great respect from the common people. Their movements have strengthened the forces of modernization as they stand for radical reorganization of society. Even these movements led to accelerate the process of land reforms, liquidation of rural indebtedness, distribution of surplus land among the rural poor, eviction of jotedari system and finally Operation Barga. On the other hand, influence of the student movements have been perhaps most pronounced in the literary and cultural life of the state.

In the context of the above study and research on the participation of the students in the socio-economic movements of West Bengal I would like to congratulate Dr. Swapan Kumar Pain for his sincere work and bringing all facts and figures in every aspect of his research work. I hope this work would receive a wide range of readership throughout the country and abroad. It will also attract the students, teachers, thinkers, policy makers and scholars alike.

Professor Anil Bhuimali
Vice Chancellor
Raiganj University
West Bengal, India

Preface and Acknowledgements

The present work is an extended version of my Doctoral Dissertation approved by the Raiganj University, West Bengal, India. This work throws light on the history of students' participation in the socio-economic issues of Bengal right from Derozian movement. Since then Bengal always exhibited a spirit of rational self-identity. A tendency to challenge what others never think twice to accept, a tendency to think ahead of others and a tendency to go on building and breaking the tradition represent. In short, it is the key to the social psychology and political temperament of Bengal.

Being a student of Modern Indian History, I came across the various socio-economic-political movements that had taken place in the different parts of our country, in which student movement was remarkable. It was not only the harvest of modern age, but also took place during the ancient and medieval period in sporadic nature. But, their characteristics had been changed from time to time. In colonial era, the student movement had its genesis in a special backdrop. They fought tooth and nail against the British imperialism since the very inception of their ascendancy. In the Post-Colonial era, there was a marked change of perspective of the student movements. It remains unabated and in many cases the movements have assumed alarming aspect. The goals of the different movements of the students, fighting in different political banners are not only political, but also social, economic, humanistic and cultural. They have embarked upon the reconstruction like unrestricted waves and have rocked seriously upon the existing political, social, economic and cultural structures. The students involved in the movements irrespective of caste, colour and creed. The movements of the students of West Bengal are no exceptions to that. The character of the movements of the students of West Bengal began changing since 1960s. Starting as nationalists they gradually assumed left and extreme ideology. The movement of the students of West Bengal at different times has been concerned with issues altering from educational problems to socio-economic issues. The quality of the movement and its socio-economic aspects had hardly been highlighted by the scholars and historians. I intend to plug this gap in my present study.

For this work, I am fortunate enough to have got an opportunity to thank and acknowledge a number of individuals who encouraged me to the completion of this study.

At the outset, I shall be failing my duty if I do not express my deep sense of gratitude to my Doctoral Supervisor Prof. Anil Bhuimali, Hon'ble Vice-Chancellor, Raiganj University, West Bengal, India. He spent much of his precious time; elucidate complex points of the research work. His encouragement was next to none. He gave me all sorts of help, suggestion, information and also academic support. His enthusiastic support and assistance have encouraged me in the preparation of my present study.

I also express my thanks and regards to Prof. Ranjan Chakrabarti, Hon'ble Vice-Chancellor, Vidyasagar University, West Bengal, India for his continuous help and support for publication of this work. I sincerely acknowledge the help extended by Prof. Projit Kumar Palit, Professor of History, Assam University, whose constant encouragement and logical thinking has given a good basis of the present study. I wish to express my thanks to Prof. Rupendra Kumar Chattopadhyay,

Vivekananda Professor of Social Science, University of Calcutta for his academic help in the way of my publication.

I also express my indebtedness to Prof. Ratna Roy Sanyal and Prof. Ananda Gopal Ghosh, former Professor of History, North Bengal University, who have been kind enough to provide many useful information, suggestion and academic support. I am also grateful to Prof. Pradip Chattopadhyay, Department of History, Burdwan University, who encouraged me to tide over the difficulties, if any, in the way of preparation of the work.

I got indirect help from the Assistant Librarian and Staff of National Library, Kolkata, State Secretariat Library, Kolkata, State Archives, Kolkata, North Bengal University Library and Uttar Dinajpur District Library. I also acknowledge the services rendered by Sri Binay Krishna Goswami of our University Library, providing me reference books and journals.

I express my indebtedness to Sri Sajal Chakraborty, Officer-In-Charge, Transport Cell, WBTDC, Kolkata, Dr. Gaur Chandra Ghosh, Associate Professor of History, and Dr. Partha Sen, Former Associate Professor of History, Islampur College, who helped me a lot to enrich the write-up. Words are not enough to my friends Goutamda, Dipak, Kasturi and Nitai, who have always inspired and assisted.

I also thank Mr. Abhishek Goel of Delta Book World for his enthusiasm and persistence in seeing this volume through the publication process.

Finally, I express my indebtedness to my wife, Smt. Jinjisa Pain (Talukdar), my child, Aniket Pain and my mother who showed infinite patience during the hours of my research work.

However, the weakness and errors that this book still contains are entirely my own responsibility.

Dr. Swapan Kumar Pain

Contents

Foreword		7
Preface and Acknowledgements		13
Abbreviations		19
1.	Introduction: Theoretical Perspective	21
2.	Evolution of Student Movement in Bengal	52
3.	Role of Students in Popular Protest Movements of Bengal (1947-1956)	83
4.	Impact of Global Student Movement: A Debate	107
5.	Role of the Students during Economic Crisis (1959-1966): The Historic Food Movement of Bengal	124
6.	Involvement of the Students in the Naxalbari Peasant Movement and After (1967-1977)	142
7.	Impact of the Movement on Contemporary Society and Economy	165
8.	Findings, Conclusions and Recommendations	174
Appendices		181
Glossary		189
Bibliography		192
Index		203

Abbreviations

ABSA	:	All Bengal Students' Association
ABPTA	:	All Bengal Primary Teachers' Association
ABTA	:	All Bengal Teachers' Association
AICSC	:	All India College Students' Conference
AISF	:	All India Students' Federation
AIMSF	:	All-India Muslim Students' Federation
AISC	:	All-India Students' Congress
BPSF	:	Bengal Provincial Students' Federation
BPSF (L)	:	Bengal Provincial Students' Federation (Left)
BPSF(R)	:	Bengal Provincial Students' Federation (Right)
CB	:	Chhatra Bloc
CP	:	Chhatra Parishad
CPI	:	Communist Party of India
CPI (M)	:	Communist Party of India (Marxist)
CPI (M-L)	:	Communist Party of India (Marxist-Leninist)
CTC	:	Calcutta Tram Company
DSO	:	Democratic Students' Organization
ICV	:	Independent Committee on Vietnam
ISA	:	Indian Students' Association
LSE	:	London School of Economics
NSU	:	National Students' Union
PSP	:	Praja Socialist Party

PSU	: Progressive Students' Union
SF	: Students' Federation
SFI	: Students' Federation of India
SA	: Socialist Association
SDS	: Students for a Democratic Society
UCRC	: United Central Refugee Council

1

Introduction: Theoritical Perspective

The students' society by all means is a part of the entire youth society. The inspirations of the youth qualities are very much prominent in the life of every student. In one side, who is a student, the same person is a youth in other side–this is the peculiar mixing of time limit in every student's life in general. During this transitional period, every good student plunged into the thinking of his future planning, expectations and demands which becomes his or, her major guidelines for achieving goals through social and educational environments. Thus, the expectation and demands of each student converted into the common hope and need for the students' society at large. The features of common thinking, expectations and demands when the students sit together, read together and stay in a common places especially in colleges, universities and other educational institutions, naturally, the flow of thinking, arguments and discussion overwhelms each other even creates an environment of common world before all students. As a result, it becomes easier to grow a unity and organizational structure automatically. Thus, when the desires and demands of students do not fulfill, as a consequence, it transforms into unrest and leading to a dissatisfied environment and agitation.

The student movement is not a current phenomenon. A number of literary sources show that it took place during the ancient and medieval period as an ongoing process of student agitation according to the time and development of the civilization. But, their movement and activities were sporadic in nature. It is very difficult to trace a movement of the students alone, rather it may be found with other sections of the society like youth, middle class intelligentsia and the teachers. At the initial stage, the reaction of the students was purely apolitical and their reaction did not take the form of movement. They had started reacting to the need of development of education system and raised various questions for mutual interests. They also showed their reaction against social rigidities, injustice and inequalities. But after the formation of political parties, the tendencies of student reaction had begun to grow politicize. It may be said that the political parties wanted to catch the budding forces. Their way of reactions were small discussions, debates, meetings, lectures and discourses, deputations, public meetings and even strikes. The abovementioned activities of the students may be considered as student movement. Gradually, it became spontaneous and organized form of movement.[1] Of course, their characteristics had been changed from time to time.

In Bengal within India, the first education system with European idealism was initiated and it was very interesting that the Indian student movement was also initiated in Bengal. The youth minds were easily attracted by the European knowledge and wisdom and by the arguments with scientific analysis.[2] Actually the British Rulers wanted that the new generation of English learning Indian would play as a weapon in favour of British administration and they should be kept alienated from the mass Indian citizens. But in History, the result was opposite. With the ideas of scientific and analytical European education, the upcoming new generation with modern learning tried to feel from the core of their hearts to hate the social superstitions and bondage of their country. This new intellectual segment or, group was originally influenced by the ingredients of freedom, fraternity and equality of the French Revolution. They were also influenced by the writings and compositions of the great philosopher and scholars like Mill, Bentham, Thomas Paine, Adam Smith etc. For example, it could be mentioned that when the books like Rights of Man by Thomas Paine, Emancipate the Colonies by Bentham reached at Kolkata from Europe, the students of the then Hindu College used to purchase those compositions then and there. In the 1st part of the 19th century, the reflection against the superstitions and injustice could be reflected on the students' movement. In spite of that influence, the students' movement could not attain a proper shape but afterwards, the flow of such student agitation was spread everywhere. This new wave of students was initiated with the pressure of Henry Louis Vivian Derozio, the young Professor of Hindu College and with the movements of Young Bengal.[3] It can be said that the neo-philosophy of life which influenced the youth intellectuals of that age afterwards shaped and ignite the flame of freedom movement among the students of that age.

The major ingredient for student movements during the Colonial Period lies within the imperialistic education system introduced by the British Rulers in India. The Britishers did not start colonial education process to enlighten the young Indian students, but they adopted it to run their imperialistic administration in India.[4] In support of their objectives, the same impression had been cleared up in the proposal of Lord Bentink in 1835 and in Macaulay's Report also. English was made the medium of higher education, under Bentinck's Resolution of 1835. Macaulay in his famous Minute said that it was impossible to educate the body of the people. A system of education was thus introduced which was prejudicial to Indian interests and enabled the British to govern the country.

It can be kept in mind that from the beginning of the twentieth century and before the starting of organized student movement, the students moved unorganized way by writing against the irregularities, bondage and conservative attitude of the British ruling. It was also observed that such student agitation against the British administration was initiated at Bengal first. The cause of such movement was to some extent for Bengal Renaissance. The student society of Bengal gradually started to feel humiliation and bondage with the expansion of the western education. In this way, the consciousness for national interest and sentiment for a common effort started to bloom in the 19th century India which takes a shape for national movement in due course day by day. Afterwards, with the advent of national movement at the beginning of 20th century, the mass student agitation converted into a national movement.[5]

In the first part of the students' movement, special emphasis was given to the constructive and cultural activities. Gradually the movement was influenced by political issues. And in the last part, the movements were influenced by the Marxist, to some extent Fascist and other political parties at large. As a result of that, the students' organizations became scattered into different wings.

All these show that the pioneers of Indian student movement never visualized the student movement as a strand by itself and disconnect from the concerns of the society at large. They sought to assimilate the students in the national movement by organizing them first on the issues that are of direct concern to them and then gradually developing their political consciousness. They were driven by an unconquerable urge to free the country from all kinds of restraints and not just the foreign rule.

Bengal's sacrifice and sufferings in pre-independence days are known to all, but in post-independence period planned exclusion of Bengal from the benefits of nation building, rapid decline of its glorious city, influx of millions of refugees, unemployment, growing economic gloom of the people have caused a sense of deprivation among the Bengalee people as also the students.[6] This is why the student movement of post-independence period which lay emphasis on the politics of protest enjoys a large following and support base in the state. The students did not participate in the socio-economic movements all of a sudden. They were to some extent stimulated by the movements of the 1960s of the USA, England, France, Germany, Italy, China, Russia and Afro-Asian countries. In addition to that the students also came to know about the facts of suffered and poverty-stricken people of the Third World which intensified the momentum of their movement. The student movement of India and particularly in West Bengal in post-independence period had lost their independent character in comparison with the student movement of European countries. Instead of their free thinking the students were more utilized by the leaders of different political parties.[7]

REVIEW OF LITERATURE

The review of literature is an integral part of any research process. It begins before a research problem is chosen and finalized. It makes valuable contribution to every operational step of the research work. At the initial stage of research, literature review may help us to clarify the ideas relating to research and enable us to develop the theoretical roots of study. The literature review can help us in four ways–

i) bring clarity and focus in understanding the research problem,

ii) to improve methodology,

iii) to extend knowledge in the proposed area, and

iv) to contextualize the findings with the existing body of knowledge.

In terms of knowledge base, the review of literature is highly acknowledged as essential. Because, it helps us to identify what has been established, and what are the gaps and inconsistencies needed to be worked out in the proposed area of research.[8] We can locate and identify the research questions and findings in the existing literature through the review process.

The review of literature has two important functions–

i) It provides a theoretical background to the area of study. In order to fulfill this purpose, we can identify and describe various theories in the relevant field and point out the research gap, recent development in the area, current trends etc. From these, we can realize that certain themes have emerged.

ii) Refining the methodology. It may help us to refine the methodology used in the process of writing. At this stage we have to wait till the research report writing stage.

In the entire review of literature, we have focused my attention around the main theme of my research i.e. "Student Participation in the Socio-Economic Movements of West Bengal in Post-Colonial Period". We have thrown light on what is already known and those unknown in the area, what questions have remained unanswered, what theories have been put forward to the area of research including the ways available for future research.

CLASSIFICATION OF REVIEW OF LITERATURE

We came across various books on methodology and review of literature. Most of these suggest four kind of literature can be reviewed i.e. Books, Journals, Conference Papers and Internet Sources. In addition to that, few other valuable historical sources are still available as potential sources of my research work. These are, in my opinion, Memoirs, Dairies,

Leaflets, Booklets, Newspapers, Magazine, Autobiographies, Anthologies, Relevant Novels and Essays. These may be added in the field of literature review. To keep in mind all these, we have tried our level best to review the literature relating to the area of research.

The literature on student movement in India is very few in number. Most of the writings have appeared in newspapers and popular periodicals and are of a journalistic nature. Historians have not explored this area. A majority of the studies have been carried out by social-psychologists, educationists, journalists, and sociologists. A few political scientists have also explored this area. Though a number of case studies on different students' agitations in the post-independence period are available, there is no comprehensive study or collected works which offers an all-India picture dealing with different types of students' agitations. We do not have any exhaustively historical account of the students' movement in India. There are a few booklets written by activists which give an account of student movements in the pre-independence period. They are vague and superficial. Vishwa Yuvak Kendra (1973) has given a list of major students' disturbances between 1947 and 1970. It provides a helpful chronology. In case of West Bengal, few books and leaflets are available which give an account on the student movement in colonial and post-colonial period.

RELEVENT LITERATURE REVIEW

The following works have sparsely thrown light on the students' movements in Colonial, Post-Colonial and Globalization phase. These works have full of information in connection with socio, economic, political, cultural and humanistic movements of the students in the different parts of our country and abroad. Some of these have written in Bengali relating to my topic closely and the rest are in English relating to vast canvas. This part also deals with the review of literature relating to various socio-economic movements of Bengal in Post-Colonial period.

Dasgupta, Hiren and Adhikary, Harinarayan (2008)[9]

This is an excellent and thought provoking book written on the basis of primary and secondary sources. The writers themselves associated with the leftist student movements in various parts of West Bengal in Post-Colonial period. From this point of view the book gets extra mileage. This book deals primarily with philosophy, organizations and movements organized by the different political parties and the students. The content of the book has been divided into three phases i.e. Colonial Phase, Post-Colonial Phase and Globalized Phase. In the Colonial Phase, the writers had given the attention to the students who fought heroically against British exploitation. They also highlighted the role of the students in the Indian National Liberation Movement. In the Post-Colonial Phase, the authors had given special emphasis on the Mass Movements of West Bengal and the participation of the students in it such as movements for civil liberty, Refugee movement, movement against Tram fare hike, Teachers' movement, anti-merger movement of West Bengal and Bihar, Food Movement which were an annual event, peasant movement, movement against national emergency etc. Side by side with the students' movements in India, the authors had focused their attention on the Globalized students' movement and their impact on India. Though, the book has so many important information on various socio-economic movement but it could not deserve the value of impartiality as because the authors themselves believed in a particular ideology.

Acharya, Anil (2014)[10]

This is a unique edited book comprising eight essays written in Bengali. Most of these essays had been published earlier in the Magazine of Anustup. The editor collected all the essays and combined those into a book. All the essays had been written by the then veteran student leader of Bengal of the 1960s and 1970s when the student movement assumed an alarming aspect in the different parts of Bengal. The writers confined their attention to the pro-Naxalite students' movement of the 1960s and 1970s. In the preface of the book, editor himself claimed that the main objective of this publication was to collect the reminiscence and appraisal of the then student leaders who were involved actively in the movement. From this point of view, it may be said that the book is not a well-researched, but very much informative. In the book, Ranabir Samaddar's essay is an excellent one. Mr. Samaddar focused the global perspective of students' movement. He highlighted the then student movements of Barlin, Rome, Stugart, Milan, London etc. and studied it comparatively with the Bengal students' movement. Another writer Saibal Mitra deals with the leftist students' movement of post-colonial Bengal up to Naxalbari Peasant Uprising. He focused mainly the socio-political movements of Bengal and how the students involved in those movements. The writer also eulogized the role of the students in the Naxalbari Movement. Asim Chatterjee wrote an article on the Students and Youths in the 60s and 70s of Bengal. The author divided his article into four phases such as post-Independence to food movement, Naxalbari movement, After Naxalbari up to the formation of CPI (M-L) and after 1969. But, he highlighted the Naxalbari phase and the participation of the students in it. Though, the book have so many important information on the various students' movement but the authors suppressed so many facts, so it could not deserve the value of proper historical documents.

Banerjee, Anirban (1998)[11]

This book contains four articles on students' movement which had been published in various journals in different times. The articles are 'Students and Politics: A Comparative

Perspective', 'The Psychology of Student Protest: A Motivational Analysis', 'The Class Character of the Student Movement: A Critique of Two Theories' and 'The Student Politics in India: A Historical Profile'. In the first article, the author has paying attention to the global student movements and its distinctiveness. He also pointed out the background of the movements at length and compared it with Indian scenario. The author chalked out the seven factors which led to the student movements such as national liberation movement, government policy, the education system, generation gap, social background, unemployment and alienation. The second article deals with the psychology of the students and their motivation that led to the different movements. The third article deals with the two major theories of student movements i.e. The New Left Theory and Generation Gap Theory. This is an ideological study. In the new left theory the student is regarded as a part of working class and the generation gap theory deals with the class consciousness. But the author was discarded both these theories by commenting that students cannot be regarded as a class, rather their consciousness based on knowledge. In the fourth article, the author highlighted the student movements in India since the Derozian movement. He divided the article into three phases such as Proto-historical phase, National Liberation Phase and Post-Independence Phase. The author has given emphasis on last two phases. He pointed out the participation of the students in the Indian Freedom Movement and the role of the students in various socio-economic movements in Post-Colonial Period like Naxalbari Peasant Movement. All these articles have been taken to highlight the movement of the students in global, ideological and Indian perspective, but it does not look particularly the movements of West Bengal.

Shah, Ghanshyam (2004)[12]

In this book Prof. Shah critically examines and reviews the literature relating to social movements in India from 1857 to present. He classified social movements into eight types on the basis of socio-economic distinctiveness such as Peasant Movements, Tribal Movements, Dalit Movements, Backward Caste Movements, Women's Movement, Working Class Movements, Students' Movements and Middle Class Movements. We have reviewed here only the Students' Movements. Dealing with the students' movement the author confines his attention to the students in colleges and universities in colonial and post-colonial period. In colonial period, he focused the involvement of the students in the National Liberation Movement. He also pointed out the role of the students in the various movements of post-colonial period. According to him the students' movements are the combinations of emotional responses and the intellectual convictions. This is a part of overall ongoing economic and political crisis in the changing nature of the social order. Unemployment is also playing a key role for students' movement. On the whole, the author chalked out the students' movement as a part of socio-economic movements. In spite of all these, the book does not have any in-depth historical account of the students' movement in India. There is no comprehensive study of all India picture dealing with different types of students' agitation.

Franda, Marcus (1971)[13]

This is an excellent and well researched book comprising eight essays on Bengal Politics. While six of these essays deal with West Bengal such as Political Development in West Bengal, The Political Idioms of Atulya Ghosh, Perceived Images of Political Authority among College Graduate in Calcutta, Electoral Politics in West Bengal: The growth of the United Front, India's Third Communist Party, and Intra-Regional Factionalism and Coalition Building in West Bengal. All the essays are intended to an analytical rather than historical interpretation of Bengal in the 1960s. The author understood the importance only in so far as relate to general questions about deep-seated political change in Bengal. First essay deals with the political consciousness in Bengal from historical background. The second one is a unique dealing with the activities of Atulya Ghosh and the renunciation of power. The third paper is a part of a larger empirical study of images of political authority among college graduates, conducted in Calcutta in 1963-1964 under the auspicious of the Ford Foundation Foreign Area Training Program. For a description of the larger research design and an elaboration of the methods used to obtain the sample. Chapter fourth highlighted the electoral politics by using primary sources. The author also focused the growth of the United Front in West Bengal, when the Congress party of West Bengal failed for the first time since Independence to gain a majority in the State. During his discussion in the Chapter, we can find out the involvement of the students in the different movements. In the Fifth and Six Chapter, Prof. Franda tried to locate the ideological differences of the communists. Though the various articles have been taken to highlight the political change in Bengal in Post-Colonial period, but it does not look particularly the changing paradigm of the student movement in Bengal.

Banerjee, Sumanta (1980)[14]

The book is a comprehensive, sympathetic and trustworthy evaluation of the political movements that began at Naxalbari in 1967. It is a history of the events which shook West Bengal, Andhra Pradesh, Punjab, Bihar, Uttar Pradesh, Orissa and many other areas throughout India in the late 1960s and early 1970s. It penetrates below the surface of the political turmoil of that period to unravel the socio-economic causes that led to the outbursts and to reassess the changes that were set in motion in the social, cultural, economic and political life of India. As a reputed journalist, the writer recorded and observed some of the facts and some are described on the basis of interviews, both with participants in the movement, and with those entrusted with the task of suppressing it. But a larger part of the book is based on theories propounded and events narrated in 'CPI (M-L) documents.

In the book one significant chapter is 'The Youth Upsurge' in which the author regarded the student movement as the intellectual ancestors of Derozio and the Young Bengal. But the author does not study the youth upsurge in grass root level. He remained silent about the socio-economic movements of the students. From his writing we find theoretical aspects only. Overall, the picture presented in this book is incomplete, obscure and inadequate. The lives of many who took part in the movement were cut short by events. Many of the key figures have died without having told the whole story. In the memory of many others, facts are often mixed with an astounding jumble of rumours, distortions and plain lies. That is why; the book may not be considered as the proper historical investigation.

Chatterjee, Partha (1997)[15]

This is an excellent and well researched book comprising fifteen essays on India's major political institutions, and analyses process of domination and resistance that play a central role in Indian politics. The book brings some landmark essays which collectively present an overall view of Indian politics as it stands, balanced on the eve of fifty years of independence. Some essays presented a picture of the growth and development of the party system, the electoral system, the federal system, planning process through the Nehru and Indra Gandhi periods etc. and the others give a sense of institutional crisis since the late 1980s. The essays deal with the political process, process of dominance by highlighting class dominance, party organization and through participatory development programmes. One of the essay entitled "From Breakdown to

Order: West Bengal" written by Atul Kohli gives a brilliant information about the socio-economic situation of West Bengal favouring left popularity. This chapter traces the roots of West Bengal's stability to the fact that a well-organized reformist party has remained in power. In the said chapter Mr. Kohli highlighted the decade of chaos from 1967 to 1977. He traced out the decline of the Congress in the mid 1960s created a power vacuum in west Bengal that was not filled until 1977. The formation of the United Front Government in 1967 led to a decade of chaos in West Bengal by two types of causes- the Naxalbari Peasant Movement and Land Grab Movement. Actually, the agrarian crisis and disputed land settlement which led to the various peasant movements. Surprisingly, Mr. Kohli did not go through the other socio-economic factors which were associated with the different political movements of the 1960s and 1970s in West Bengal.

Chakrabarti, Prafulla Kumar (1999)[16]

The book is a significant original work which carried out comprehensive basic research and integrated much of information. It is a remarkable application of the Marxian tools of historical analysis and understanding of the nature and characteristics of various classes. Though, it is a comprehensive history of the refugees from East Pakistan and of their impact of the body politic of West Bengal, but the reader gets so many information of the socio-economic conditions of the then Bengal. The Marginal Men argues that the organization, United Central Refugee Council (UCRC), transformed the traditional and conformist West Bengal society into one with a fundamental and modernized ideology. The UCRC succeeded in mobilizing the refugees under its banner. Its organizational machinery became the basic infrastructure of all future left agitation in West Bengal. In the book, there is a vast chapter on Food Movement of West Bengal and the involvement of the students and teen-agers in it. Author argued that food was the one problem which was not exclusively for refugees. It was affected the entire people of West Bengal. To the left opposition it was an issue which offered great possibilities. The food movement was an annual affair and it got highest height in 1959 and the involvement of the students and teen-agers were spectacular in the movement. There was a students' strike in protest against the police action on food agitators and even the teen-agers forced many school to close. In spite of all these, the book does not have any in-depth historical account of the students' participation in the food movement in Bengal. The author avoids the movement which took place in the northern part of Bengal. There was huge refugee influx and movements happened including food grains and students' movement regarding food took a violent shape in Coochbehar. There is no comprehensive study of all Bengal picture dealing with different types of agitation.

Ehrenreich, Barbara & John (1969)[17]

The book deals with the student movement held in Germany, France, Italy, England and the United States of America in the late 1960s. The spring of 1968 witnessed an unprecedented outbreak of student demonstration and revolt in Western Europe and the United States. The May Uprising in France, triggered by the students and joined by millions of workers, which brought that nation to the threshold of revolution, and the dramatic seizure in April of five buildings by Columbia University students, made headlines all over the world. At the same time students in Germany and Italy battled in the streets with police and occupied University buildings. The book was written mainly on the basis of interviews with the participants who were actively involved in the movement. The authors critically evaluated the growth of the student movement and projected its future perspective in various chapters. They highlighted the Columbia University students' movement. The chapter deals with German and Italian uprising had good historical information in connection with the student movement. In concluding chapter, the authors pointed out the general theory of student activism. But the authors are not highly successful in producing a theory which covers both the European and American scene. The writers remained silent about the assumption of the revolutionaries. The authors did not highlight the impact of the movement on the society and economy at large.

Chakraborty, Shyamal (2011)[18]

The book has been written on the basis of writer's own experiences as because the writer was a prominent student leader of that period keeping touched with the mass movements of Bengal. The author wrote that the student movement of the 1960s and 1970s was marked as the enlightened episode in the history of democratic movement in West Bengal. Though the title of the book is student movements of the 1960s and 1970s, but the facts and incidents have been described from the 1950s and continued up to 1967. In the 1950s, the author highlighted the participation and active role of the leftist students in the movement of civil liberty, movement against communal violence, refugee movement, movement against the hike of Tram fare, active participation of the students in the Teachers' movement, anti-merger movement of West Bengal and Bihar, Food movement etc. The writer eulogizes the role of the leftist students in those movements. In the 60s, the student movement got its highest height with the influence of global student movement especially the westernized student movement, which pointed out by the author in the preface of his book, but it was not written in the Pratham Khanda or First Part. The unique character of the book is a noteworthy mentioning of the then literary and cultural side. According to the author without mentioning the literary and cultural works of the then Bengal, the writing of the history of the student movement will be incomplete. This is really a positive sense of history writing.

Apart from all these, the writer himself claimed that it may not be a complete history as because there was scarcity of sources which is essential for history writing. The author also stepped to relate the student movement of the then society, economy and culture in the background. It is observed that the author named the book 60-70 Er Chhatra Andolan, but he mentioned the movements of the leftist students only. Another important point is that the author himself believed in a particular ideology, so it may not be a proper description of the facts. But the conscious reader may get lot of information from this book and verify it from other sources. It is better to say that the book is a reminiscence and appraisal of the author.

Guha Roy, Siddhartha (1990)[19]

This is a unique and excellent article written by Dr. Siddhartha Guha Roy. The article mainly focused on the Calcutta Tram Fare Movement and its background. In the article, the writer vividly discussed the socio-economic perspective of the Tram workers and the sympathy of the general people towards them. The author used the views of a British Tramcar specialist namely Dennis Gill, the views of Eric Hobsbawm, the then ruling Government, the opposition parties, the role of students and the reporting of various Newspapers in his whole writing. According to author Riots and insurrections have been part of Calcutta's history and one of the interesting features of crowd action in the city, before and since independence, is the attack on tramcars by frenzied mobs. This paper attempts to capture the urban disturbance and mob violence that erupted in Calcutta in 1953 in the wake of a sudden rise in second class tram fares and studies the tramway men's attitude towards people's protest as also the reaction of the West Bengal government to the episode.

Dealing with the role of students, the author wrote, a new aspect of the movement was mass involvement of the students of Calcutta. The interference of the police force and detain of several students gave the demonstration a more aggressive shape. He also pointed out the facts which happened in Ashutosh College in South Calcutta. The police entered the college and resorted to severe torture. This added fuel to the fire and then the students throughout the city created demonstration over tramcars. The author said, after this incident the students and the citizens of Calcutta organised a massive demonstration before the head office of the Tramcar. Overall, the views of author, the Calcutta trams played a leading role in generating a mass movement in Calcutta. In fact, small economic issue of fare rise was made the basis of a large-scale challenge to the forces of law and order. The fight against fare rise was essentially a struggle against British capital. But the entire tide of mass resentment finally went also against the Congress government of West Bengal. One significant weapon used by the demonstrators of the Tram fare movement was the leaflets, poetry, songs etc., which had influenced the society to some extent. The writer avoided this part, but he completed all aspects of the movement using proper references.

Acharya, Anil (2014)[20]

This is a well-marked edited book comprising ten essays on social, economic and political movements of West Bengal of 1970s. All essays are intended to present reminiscence, rather than historical interpretation of Bengal at that time. In the Post-Colonial history of Bengal, the 60s and 70s was marked as the episode of resistance. Side by side, there was a debate among the scholars about the nature of that resistance movement. But the scholars agreed these resistance movement of Bengal rocked the entire socio-economic system of India. The editor relentlessly collected the essays from those who were to some extent loyal to the agitators. In the present study, the editor had given special emphasis on the society and economy of Bengal of the 1970s.

The first essay was written by Samar Sen on Sattar Dashaker Chalchitra. He presented an all India picture of that time. The second article was written by Sumanta Banerjee on Naxalbari Andolan O Sattar Dashak. Here, the writer presented the Naxalbari movement as anti-feudal and against exploitation. He also gave a vivid description of the student participation in the movement. According to him, the students were influenced by the then westernized student movement. The third essay was written by Mahasweta Devi on Sattar Dashak O Tarpar, and in this the author pointed out the deplorable condition of tribal people and how they were exploited by the feudal lords. The fourth article was written by Badaruddin Umar on Sattar Dashaker Krishak Andolan. He gave a detailed description of the peasant movement from 1947 to 1977. Above all, the writers focused anti-establishment character of the different movement.

In spite of all these, the book does not have any in-depth historical account of the socio-economic movements of the seventies. Most of the authors consciously or unconsciously avoided the proper historical sources in their writing. But, the overall writing will be helpful for further research.

Shah, Ghanshyam (2012)[21]

This work examines the social movements of India as a defining force in the political process. It reviews an extra-institutional collective action as agents of political and social change. The book covers social movements of India over the last five decades. In the different essays, the authors have focused on three aspects; why the movements took place, what were the main elements and how the state responds to various forms of collective action?

All the writers tried to discuss the various definitions of social movement first and examine the growing movement in the different parts of India. According to them, these movements were the result of institutional failure and the growing aspirations of the masses. As a result, various protests, agitations, strikes and riots were developed. The authors covered the rise and growth of various peasant, tribal, women and student movements in Colonial and Post-Colonial period.

In the present work, dealing with the essay written by Sumanta Banerjee on 'Naxalbari and the Left Movement', discussed in details about left movement and their fraction, ideological differences, path of action and the role of first United Front Government in West Bengal. Then writer had given special emphasis on the student participation in the peasant movement of Naxalbari. Though the movement started in Naxalbari area of Derjeeling district and the students of North Bengal University and adjoining Siliguri College were there, but gradually the movement shifted from North to South especially the focal point of the student movement was the then Presidency College and Calcutta University. According to author, the Naxalbari movement left a far-reaching impact on the students at that time. But the writer did not enter into deep. A section of students participated in the Naxalbari Peasant Movement; few of them are still surviving. Only the surviving student can tell us their actual role in the movement. Apart from all these, the work is informative, which may help for future research.

Liberation Anthology (1992)[22]

This Anthology presents a selection of writings from Liberation, which appeared from its inception in November 1967 to early 1972. Liberation was the central organ of the All India Co-Ordination Committee of Communist Revolutionaries (AICCCR) that was set up in the wake of the Naxalbari uprising in 1967, and of the Communist Party of India (Marxist-Leninist) after the dissolution of the AICCCR. This Anthology includes a number of documents and other writings of historical importance not published in Liberation or elsewhere. The old copies of Liberation are not available. This Anthology can supply the partial source material on the history of that period.

In the Anthology, an article has been found on 'To the Youths and the Students' written by Charu Majumder, the architect of the Naxalbari Peasant Movement, which was published in Liberation in April, 1969. In the said article, the writer used a quotation of Mao-Tse-Tung to insist the students as widely as possible for taking extremist path. The quotation is "...there can only be one criterion by which we should judge whether a youth or a student is a revolutionary. This criterion is whether or not he is willing to integrate himself with the broad masses of workers and peasants, does so in practice and carries on mass work." In the same article, the author had highly emphasized the participation of the youths and students in the peasant and worker movement. The students fought in the barricade over some student demand or economic and political issues. The writer advised the students that the political organization of the youths and students must necessarily be a Red Guard Organization, and they should undertake the task of spreading the quotation of Mao-Tse-Tung.

In the present writing, the author clearly hinted the students to take the revolutionary path. Actually, the writer provoked the students by way of writing. But, we found that a section of students were involved in the extremist movement. A Large section of the students were kept aloof from the extremist activities. We hope with all its shortcomings these writings or this anthology may be a source of information of that period. But it should be verified from other primary sources for reconstructing impartial writing.

Chatterjee, Rakhahari (1985)[23]

In the present work of Prof. Rakhahari Chatterjee, ten political scientists examines different aspects of West Bengal politics from 1947 to 1980.The contributors to this volume have adopted the simple descriptive and analytical approach in assessing the politics of West Bengal. Most of the contributors have focused the Post-Independence crisis which affects the political forces of West Bengal. It is marked that, since independence West Bengal has been passing through serious economic, social and political crises.

In the present book, the writers made an attempt to explain lucidly how the congress declined and emerged the left political force, what are the problems of the left, why did the Naxalite Movement develop and decline, how the workers and peasants tried to cope with changing situation etc. Their way of discussion and simplicity of approach should make this book enjoyable. In every essay, the authors have used a strong reference, which gives extra mileage of this book.

In the book, one significant article was written by Prof. Apurba Mukhopadhyay on "The Left in West Bengal: Government and Movement, 1967-1982". In the said article, an attempt is made to sum up the experiences of communist and the left political activities in West Bengal from 1967 to 1980. At the very beginning, the author explained in detail the background of left extremist movement started from North Bengal. In this Movement, the students and youths played a vital role in favour of the peasants. According to author, like all socio-political movements, it also was a child of history. In the second phase of discussion, it was noticed that after 1972 when the economic crisis was going on, the students and youths of West Bengal sprang up against rising prices, food shortage, high unemployment and Government corruption. Like West Bengal, the Gujrat and Bihar also faced strong student movement on the same ground. One significant thing, noticed in the writings, that the socio-economic background of West Bengal, which is most important for presenting anything of that tumultuous period. Otherwise, the entire work is interesting for knowing first political change of West Bengal.

Mukherjee, Arun Prasad (2007)[24]

This is an important account of the complexities of the entire Naxalite Movement, covering the two major episodes—i) the movement of the Naxalbari areas during 1967-68 and ii) the later phase of 1969-72 affecting Calcutta and its adjoining areas. The author wrote this book on the basis of unknown Government and police records of the entire period, with interesting explanatory notes. In the book, the detailed interrogation statements of Asim Chatterjee, Souren Bose, Kanu Sanyal, Sadhan Sarkar, Nishit Bhattacharjee, Nagbhusan Patnaik, Shyamal Kumar Ghosh and Charu Majumder have been incorporated, which revealed the strength and weakness of the movement. Apart from the historical value of these interrogation reports, they also depict the developments of the movement as seen through the eyes of the leading figures. These also revealed the inner contradictions, mutual suspicions, attempts at self-exculpation and the pervading atmosphere of terror within the party, even among leading members prevented them or others from expressing their dissenting views for fear of liquidation by their own comrades. From pages 258 to 267, a comprehensive statement given by Asim Chatterjee, was laid down, in which the researcher may find out lots of information relating to extremist student movement of the then Presidency College and other adjoining colleges and universities.

As the author had occasion not only to deal with the challenges of the movement but had also developed personal rapport with many of its principal leaders, this document based narrative has the unmistakable flavor of authenticity coupled with deep understanding of the major issues involved. The distressing and persistent lack of understanding of the major issues on the part of the Governmental authorities in dealing with the current phase of the movement has been brought out forcefully in the author's introductory notes which deserve a close look. The author's analytical view of the two phases movement brings to fore many unknown facts of those tumultuous years.

Being an IPS officer, the author was the then posted as Superintendent of Police in Darjeeling District and Naxalbari falls under this district. As head of the district police, he prepared so many important documents and reports of the time relating to various events comprising the Naxalite Movement and sent it to the Government. At the same time he collected few rare photographs of the movements and incorporated the same in this book, which have intrinsic historical interest. These should also help in correcting many distorted accounts which came out later.

The author wrote this book on the basis of police records and his own experiences. From this point of view the book gets an extra mileage as because it depends full of primary sources. On the other hand the author knowingly or unknowingly avoided the secondary sources like contemporary news papers, views of local people; eye witness etc. If the author may include these sources in writing, his work will be complete one. Apart from all these, the book is informative one for the future research.

Basu, Sibaji Pratim (2016)[25]

Dr. Basu's work entitled 'The Chronicle of a Forgotten Movement: 1959 Food Movement Revisited' was one of the most significant instances of mass movements in West Bengal. He compared these movements with Charles Tilly's conceptions of 'contentious politics' and 'social movements' which originated in Europe in the eighteenth century and broaden all over the World in the following centuries through colonialism, trade and migration. He also found certain 'rhizomatic' tendencies – a term borrowed from Deluze and Guattari – in these movements as they evinced creation of their own structures and functions without much contribution from the 'vertical leadership.' The author contextualized the Food Movement of 1959 in the backdrop of the famine in Bengal in 1943, the consequent peasant mobilizations in the late 1940s and the corrupt and inadequate public distribution system in post-independence West Bengal. The failure of the government to secure and distribute food grains together with the increasing population pressure after partition led to massive hoarding and black marketing which synthetically increased the food price. The opposition leaders of Bengal took a twine policy in this regard. They brought the issue of food paucity inside the State Assembly and thereby, drew public and media attention. Secondly, as a tactic of organizing anti-government mass movements, they formed various issue-based committees like the Price Increase and Famine Resistance Committee (PIFRC) for broader public support. The PIFRC had played a historic role during the food movement.

The author pointed out that the common people wanted rice to be seized from the hoarded stocks of the big stockiest and dealers and sold through government or semi government agents at reasonable price. According to him the 1959 Food Movement gave birth to three kinds of reaction: (1) an angry reaction against the government's handling of the situation; (2) blaming the organizers of the movement for indulging in 'lawless anarchy'; (3) a balanced assessment which criticized both the government's food policy and its handling of the situation and the left leadership's losing control over the situation.

In the said work, Dr. Basu opined that the food movement of 1959 was continued to vibrate in public memory and culminated in 1966 in a more furious food movement where the onus shifted from the state capital of Calcutta to the districts.

One thing could be noticed in the paper that the author did not touch the movements of the North Bengal, where the food movement got momentum especially in Coochbehar District. He also avoided how the left parties earned the people's trust by utilizing these movements. Otherwise, the work is unique one covering different aspects of the movement.

Banerjee, Paula (2016)[26]

The literature on refugees has followed a certain common trend. Dealing with, it was a literature of victimhood in which the refugees were portrayed only as victims. It cannot be denied that in large parts these refugees were victims but even as victims they constantly tried to negotiate with power structures as agents. The cultural studies in West Bengal the refugee experience was condensed to the memory of the refugees. Historians like Dipesh Chakrabarty, discussed the inventive mappings of the refugee lives expressed through memories. These writings did not contradict the victimhood narrative but added a new dimension to it. Apart from these, there are other historians who have tried to understand refugee experience through experiences of particular communities. Authors like Shekhar Bandyopadhyay and Joya Chatterjee belongs to these schools of thought. The shape of the partition refugee in West Bengal is now a favourite theme of research for many scholars. One such aspect is how the refugee movement became part of the popular movements in West Bengal in the 1950s and 1960s. Most of these authors have not tried to depict its connections with movement against eviction, land riots, food movements, or the women's movement. Banerjee's work will fill up this gap. The other objective of her research is to build up a collection that will include relevant documents regarding the refugee movement in West Bengal and the role that the refugees played in other popular movements. This collection will contain speeches of leaders and politicians on the issue and all documents that are in the public sphere, notwithstanding far from public access. It will also enclose newspaper reports, police reports, government documents and these documents will have an annotated bibliography pointing to the archival material that contributes to this description. The author proved in her paper how one movement disposed and displaced many other movements. But the author stressed more focus on archival records, though her work should not be confined to it.

The abovementioned literatures have thrown light on the various socio-economic-political movements of Bengal as well as India and the movements of the students. These literatures help us to clarify the ideas of research and to plug the gap of research.

OBJECTIVES OF THE STUDY

What is being studied in the course of the present research are as follows:

i) To give a historical account of the growth and development of student movement in Bengal.

ii) To examine the origin of the Students' Organization and their divisions.

iii) To overview the socio-economic situation of Bengal favouring the emergence of Student movement.

iv) To locate the role of students in the socio-economic movements of Bengal

v) To highlight the difficulties faced by students.

vi) To judge the policies of the then Governments from which the students gained popularity.

vii) To find out the genesis of Oppression of the Governments and ruling class upon the students' organization.

RESEARCH GAP

A number of research works have been done on the Students Movements and its influence on national and international level but the proper investigation into the participation of the students in the socio-economic movements of West Bengal has never been undertaken. It is perhaps high time to investigate their involvement in the movements from academic point of view. There is a need to highlight the facts and truths in the light of recent available documents. This dissertation would be an outcome of such an academic exercise.

RESEARCH QUESTIONS

In connection with the abovementioned objectives the following research questions have been framed for testing:

1. Why did the students involve in the Mass Movements?
2. What was the historical background of the Mass Movements?
3. How did the students organize themselves before they became popular?
4. Why did common men and intelligentsia feel attracted to the students?
5. Was there any connection of the movement with the contemporary global students' movement?
6. What was the magnitude of the contribution in the fields of Society and economy?
7. What is the relevance of the movements today?

METHODOLOGY OF RESEARCH

1. The basic methodological approach for this research is paradigmatic.
2. It is based on empirical deductive principles.
3. In the composition of the paradigm though the basic element is historical, it will nevertheless be a multi-disciplinary approach incorporating the dependent variables from Political Science, Economics and Sociology.
4. Field Survey and Personal Interviews have also been important.

CHAPTER PLAN

To understand the student participation in the socio-economic movements of Bengal fully, we have to divide the entire work into eight chapters such as:

(i) Introduction: Theoretical Perspective,

(ii) Evolution of Student Movement in Bengal,

(iii) Role of Student in Popular Protest Movements in Bengal (1947-1956),

(iv) Impact of Global Student Movement: A Debate,

(v) Role of the Student During Economic Crisis (1959-1966): The Historic Food Movement of Bengal,

(vi) Involvement of the Students in the Naxalbari Peasant Movement and After (1967-1977),

(vii) Impact of the Movement on Contemporary Society and Economy, and

(viii) Findings, Conclusion and Recommendation.

NOTES AND REFERENCES

1. Rajimwale, Anil (2001), History of Student Movement in India: Origins and Development (1920-1947), Manak Publications Pvt. Ltd., New Delhi, pp.2-3.
2. Khai Thrombosis, *Bharatkosa (1967)* (In Bengali), Vol. III, *Bangiya Sahitya Parisad,* Kolkata, p. 409.
3. Sarkar Susobhan (1970), Bengal Renaissance and Other Essays, People's Publishing House, New Delhi, p. 11.
4. Dasgupta, H. and Adhikary, H.(1993 & 2008), Rajnaitik Poto Bhumite Bharatiya Upamahadesher Chhatra Andolan(In Bengali), School for People, Medinipore, and Radical Impression, Kolkata, p. 366.
5. Pain, S. K. (2017), Growth and Development of the Student Movement of Bengal: Unorganised to Organised, published by The Quarterly Review of Historical Studies, Vol. LVI, No. 3 & 4, IHS, Kolkata, pp. 87-88.

6. Ray, S. (2007): Marxist Parties of West Bengal: 1947-2001, Progressive, Kolkata, p. 35.
7. Ghosh, Shyamal Kumar (2014), Naxalite Student-Youth Movement of 1970, Sopan Publisher, Kolkata, p. 119.
8. Kumar Ranjit (2014), Research Methodology, Sage Publications Pvt. Ltd., New Delhi, p. 48.
9. Dasgupta, H. and Adhikary H. (1993 & 2008): Rajnaitik Poto Bhumite Bharatiya Upamahadesher Chhatra Andolan (in Bengali), Published by Chandi Samanta, School for Peoples' Emancipation, Medinipore and Radical Impression, Kolkata.
10. Acharya, Anil (ed, 2008 & 2014): Shat-Sattarer Chhatra Andolan (in Bengali), Anustup, Kolkata, Revised and Enlarged Edition, 2014.
11. Banerjee, Anirban (1998): Exploring Student Politics, Published by Manasi Banerjee, Burdwan, West Bengal.
12. Shah, Ghanshyam (2004): Social Movements in India, Sage Publication Pvt. Ltd., New Delhi.
13. Marcus, Franda F. (1971): Political Development and Political Decay in Bengal, Massachusetts Institute of Technology, and Firma K. L. M., Kolkata.
14. Banerjee, Sumanta (1980): In the Wake of Naxalbari, Subarnarekha, Kolkata.
15. Chatterjee, Partha (ed, 1997): State and Politics in India, Oxford University Press, Delhi.
16. Chakrabarti, Prafulla Kumar (1999): The Marginal Men, Naya Udyog, Kolkata.
17. Barbara, E. and John, E. (1969): Long March, Short Spring: The Student Uprising at Home and Abroad, First Modern Paperback Edition, U.S.A.
18. Chakraborty, S. (2011): 60-70 Er Chhatra Andolan, Pratham Khanda (in Bengali), National Book Agency, Kolkata.
19. Guha Roy, Siddhartha (1990): Fare Hike and Urban Protest, Calcutta Crowd in 1953, Published in Economic and Political Weekly, December 29, 1990.

20. Acharya, Anil (ed, 2014): Sattar Dasak: A Socio-economic Political and Cultural evaluation of the Seventies, Pratham Khanda (in Bengali), Anustup, Kolkata, Revised and Enlarged Edition.
21. Shah, Ghanshyam (ed. 2012): Social Movements and the State, Vol. IV, Sage Publications, New Delhi, Fifth Edition, 2012.
22. Liberation Anthology (1992), Vol. I, edited by Suniti Kumar Ghosh and Associates, Published by S. K. Ghosh, Calcutta.
23. Chatterjee, Rakhahari (Ed. 1985): Politics in West Bengal; Institutions, Processes and Problems, The World Press Pvt. Ltd., Calcutta.
24. Mukherjee, Arun Prasad (2007): Maoist Spring Thunder: The Naxalite Movement (1967-1972), K. P. Bagchi & Company, Kolkata.
25. Basu, Sibaji Pratim (2012): Food Movements of 1959 and 1966, Seminar Proceedings titled "Popular Movements in West Bengal and Bihar", Dated. 28.02.2016, Kolkata, Found at *www.mcrg.ac.in* and Basu's article entitled "The Chronicle of a Forgotten Movement: 1959 Food Movement Revisited", 2012.
26. Banerjee, Paula (2012): Refugee Movement in West Bengal, Seminar Proceedings titled "Popular Movements in West Bengal and Bihar".

2

Evolution of Student Movement in Bengal

It is not at all irrelevant to say that student movement is not only the harvest of Modern Age, but also has clear evidence which took place during the ancient and medieval period as an ongoing process of student agitation according to the time and development of the civilization. There is a common proverb in Sanskrit "Chhatranang Adhayanang Topo" (learning is Students' motto) – which signifies the training and practice of disciples in the House of the Teacher or Gurukul system. We can see many incidents of education and learning of disciples in the house of teacher in ancient India especially during the Vedic Age.[1] Like India, similar incidents also took place in Western Countries. Researchers have studied on this matter earlier and even they have been engaging themselves to explore more information on this issue.

The great scholar Patanjali in the 1st and the 2nd century B.C. had mentioned similar types of several incidents in the book named Mahavashya, in which we can see the good number of student movements. The students in the Ashrama of Panini were more attentive to know about the learning of their livelihood rather than to gather knowledge for education. Many students were more interested to join for mixing with the girl students or, with the damsels who resided in the Ashrama of 'Dakshya' or, in the Ashrama where such unmarried girls' students were continuing their studies. Among the students some were more interested to join Rudhir Ashrama as Patanjali described as 'butter or ghee' and such group of pupil was known as 'Ghrita Rudhira'. According to Panini there were some students who were very much idle in nature and often wasted their valuable time by sleeping and they were known as 'Khatwa-Aruha'. Beside this, Panini described that there were some group of pupil who often changed their Ashramas and they were also called as 'Tirtha-Kaka'. For such behaviour and abnormality the students' society became much indiscipline segment in that society. According to the Great Greek scholar Socratis, Students' resentment became a worldwide condition which was a long time problems that revealed depending upon the magnitude of time and situation.[2]

Ayodhya Kando of Ramayana composed by Valmiki, several agitations of unruly students could be traced who never followed the rules and regulations of their dwelling places in different Ashramas. Even, the similar occurrences also could be found in the composition of 'Uttara Ramcharittam' by Bhavabhuti, published in 17th century and such type of unruly students were known as 'Sandhataki'.[3]

After observing the student movement during the ancient and middle ages it may be said that there were various types of social irregularities during that time which led to an agitation by the students. The behaviour and temperaments of Brahmin Gurus or, Teachers of the then society to the general students or, disciples for their hatred, neglect and inhuman dealings towards non-Brahmin pupil created a remarkable difference with each other, which led to racism and communalism in the minds of students. In this way, in India and in other countries of the World, from the ancient and middle age, the students' movement originated and rolled out depending upon the time and reality in different ages.[4] The policies, desires and patterns of the ruling set up during the Modern Age also nurtured the education systems, which also influenced the educational environment. It reflects the impression and image of the existing administrative machinery as a whole. For that very reason, the background of students' movement was more and more important.

STUDENT MOVEMENT IN THE 19TH CENTURY

The students' movement of the 19th century had its genesis in a special backdrop. The movements were allowed to develop in the firmament of the movement of the Indian masses against the British imperialism. The socio-economic condition of India was passing through serious vicissitudes at a time when the British were in the struggle for the establishment of an empire in India. The British established its far-flung empire in India taking advantage of the decadent stage of the Mughal Empire. The heyday of the Mughal Empire had gone. Thereafter, the British administration as also the British exploitation was started. But the people of India could not evenly accept the British Rule. They fought tooth and nail against the British Rule since the very inception of their ascendancy. The students of India stepped into the shoes of freedom fighters of the subcontinent.[5]

At the beginning of the 19th century the students and its leadership have begun playing a determined and major role in social change. But, it is very difficult to trace a movement of the students alone. They are usually to be found with the various other sections of youth, middle class and the rising Bengali intelligentsia. After the introduction of modern education a fresh consciousness gradually brought the educated youth in contact with the modern events in various parts of the country and the world at large. They started to pay attention to the problems facing the country and the people and to look upon them in different light. The ideas of the French Revolution, writings and compositions of the great philosopher and scholars like Mill, Bentham, Thomas Paine, David Ricardo, Adam Smith etc, the movements in the Italian Peninsula, and other events became tremendous source of inspiration for the students and youth to think and to do something new. The preliminary reaction of the students was not political nor did it take the form of movement, they began reacting to the needs of better and wider education, social change, to spread and share the newly acquired consciousness and social reforms. Gradually, political tendencies also begin to surface.[6] They are usually to be found with the various other sections of youth, middle strata and the rising intelligentsia. The growing student unrest in India constitutes the social context in recent past. This unrest of the students may not be entirely new to western countries, but considering the sacred status of the guru in ancient India, it is certainly new to us.[7] The explanations of student unrest given by different academician, scholars and journalists are the psychological, psychoanalytical and sociological. Ross (1969) classifies students' protests into five categories:

(1) Political protests;
(2) Economic protests;
(3) Moral protests;
(4) Educational protests; and
(5) Protests for fun.

These protests are often interconnected. There are certain factors which are found in all types of protests. According to many sociologists and social psychologists one common factor of all types of students' protests is the 'generation gap'. In a transitional and pluralistic society, it is difficult for students to conform to establish norms.[8]

The major ingredient for student movements during the Colonial Period lies within the imperialistic education system introduced by the British Rulers in India. The Britishers did not start colonial education process to enlighten the young Indian students, but they adopted it to run their imperialistic administration in India.[9] In support of their objectives, the same impression had been cleared up in the proposal of Lord Bentinck in 1835 and in Macaulay's Report also. English was made the medium of higher education, under Bentinck's Resolution of 1835. Macaulay in his famous Minute said that it was impossible to educate the body of the people. A system of education was thus introduced which was prejudicial to Indian interests and enabled the British to govern the country.

In the early stage of the 19th century the problems related with the social reforms were the focal point of students' agitation. This consciousness of the students was one of the consequences of modern system of western education introduced by the colonial masters. This insisted the educated youth conscious about the social, economic and religious inequalities, discriminations and orthodoxies. These social evils led to the serious reaction among the educated middle class or the Bhadraloke class and students exemplified more comprehensibly in the ideas of Raja Rammohan Roy, Derozio and Young Bengal and several other streams. The primary reaction of the educated youth and students was not only political, but also social, humanistic and cultural. Their reaction did not take the shape of movement in modern form. They began reacting to the needs of better and wider education, social change, discussions on various questions of mutual interests, to spread and share the newly acquired knowledge and consciousness and to protest against various kinds of injustices.[10] But, gradually their protests began to come into sight with certain political tendencies.

BIRTH OF ACADEMIC ASSOCIATION

In Bengal within India, the first education system with European idealism was initiated and it was very interesting that the Indian student movement was also initiated in Bengal. The youth minds were easily attracted by the European knowledge and wisdom and by the arguments with scientific analysis.[11]

Actually the British Rulers wanted that the new generation of English learning Indian would play as a weapon in favour of British administration and they should be kept alienated from the mass Indian citizens. But in history, the result was opposite. With the ideas of scientific and analytical European education, the upcoming new generation with modern learning tried to feel from the core of their hearts to hate the social superstitions and bondage of their country. This new intellectual segment or, group was originally influenced by the ingredients of freedom, fraternity and equality of the French Revolution. They were also influenced by the writings and compositions of the great philosopher and scholars. For example, it could be mentioned that when the books like Rights of Man by Thomas Paine, Emancipate the Colonies by Bentham reached at Calcutta from Europe, the students of the then Hindu College used to purchase those compositions then and there. In the 1st part of 19th century, the reflection against the superstitions and injustice was seen on the students' movement. In spite of that influence, the students' movement could not attain a proper shape but afterwards, the flow of such student agitation was spread everywhere. This new wave of students was initiated with the inspiration of Henry Louis Vivian Derozio (18 April, 1809-26 December, 1831), the young professor of Hindu College and with the movements of Young Bengal. In one side he was a teacher and on the other, he was their friend. He was a Calcutta Eurasian Portuguese Indian ancestry, the son of an officer in an English Mercantile Firm. His name is occasionally spelt as De Rozio. His personality brought a new era in the annals of the college, the youthful teacher drawing the senior boys like a magnet. According to his biographer "neither before, nor since his day has any teacher, within the walls of any native educational establishment in India, ever exercised such an influence over his pupils not only in classrooms, but also outside the hours as well." In 1828, after a constructive discussion, the formation of Academic Association took shape in the House of Derozio.[12] Derozio was its first president and Uma Charan Basu, student of Derozio, was its first secretary. The students of Derozio were the forerunner of this mission. It was the first student organization in India functioning in an organized and regular manner.[13]

The vibrant factor behind the rise of academic association was the growing modern consciousness termed as renaissance among a section of educated Bengali people. This section of the people was well acquainted to the social problems. They were frustrated with the social discrimination in terms of caste, classes, sex, religion, tradition etc. They also showed their dissatisfaction to the exploitative nature of the British rule.[14] It may be said that this consciousness among the educated people was the byproduct of western education and other movements of European countries and subsequently they reacted against the social injustice and discrimination. These new consciousness had left a deep impact on the radical students and they thought to be organized. Derozio organized these students and trained them to fight against the orthodox practices. He persistently encouraged students to free thinking, to question and not to believe anything blindly. His teachings inspired the development of the spirit of liberty, equality and freedom.

To spread the aims and objectives of newly formed Academic Association, the students of Derozio took an effort to publish one Magazine named Parthenon in 1829 and finally it was published in 1830. The worship to idols, superstitions were highly criticized and objected through this publication and it influenced the people in favour of spreading the scientific education. In support of the success of the July Revolution of 1830, some students of the then Hindu College wanted to greet that movement and they hoisted the Flag of French Revolution on the top of the Monument which carried the impressions of equality, friendship and freedom and replaced the Union Jack of the British Emperor. Prof. Susobhan Sarkar (1979) opined that 200 students attended the July Revolution celebration in the Town Hall, Kolkata on10th December, 1830. For such an incident and protest by the reactionaries, Derozio was compelled to leave the Hindu College. But in spite of expulsion of Derozio, the new wave of conscious thinking could not be wiped out from the mind of the students.[15] It can be said that the neo-philosophy of life which influenced the youth intellectuals of that age afterwards shaped and ignite the flame of freedom movement among the students of that age.

ACTIVITIES OF THE ACADEMIC ASSOCIATION

The prominent members of the Academic Association were Krishna Mohan Banerjee, Rasik Krishna Mallick, Peary Chand Mitra, Dakshina Ranjan Mukherjee, Radhanath Sikdar, Hara Chandra Ghosh, Tarinicharan Banerjee, Ramtanu Lahiri, Tarachand Chakraborty, Ramkrishna Dey, Ramgopal Ghosh, Uma Charan Basu who believed classical economy and free trade. These radical students were very critical to the social, economic and political problems of the period. Their main task was to arrange discussion on the matter such as free will, the sacredness of truth, patriotism, free ordination, debate on burning issues etc. The discussion of the academic association attracted the attention of the educated elites of Bengal and even English administrators. For example, David Hare, Col. Benson, private secretary of Lord William Bentinck were regularly present to their discussion.[16] They also discussed to the need of female education and introduction of widow remarriage and published articles on the subject regularly.

The radical student movement of 1830s fought against all kinds of social problems. It played a noteworthy role in the spheres of social activities. The pioneer of this movement was Derozians. The students of academic association were vehemently criticised the Hindu orthodox practices. They indulged in prohibited food and drink. Some of the students used to repeat lines from Iliad instead of mantras at the time of prayer in Hindu College. Even, they used to take beef openly. These activities showed the extreme and revolting attitude to the tradition. A thorough revolution took place in their ideas.[17] They raised their voice against the forced labour, introduction of English as court language, press act, political power of the company, and unprotected status of the peasantry.[18] They also agitated by the issues like treatment of Indian labour in Mauritius, the extension of the right of trial by jury, the introduction of English as court language, freedom of press and forced labour amongst the coolies employed by various government departments.[19] Their main weapon of protest was small discussions, debates, meetings, hall gatherings, lectures and discourses, petition and protest letters, public meetings and even strikes. Their strongest weapon of publicity was various newspapers, periodicals and journals which discussed below in details.

PUBLICATIONS OF THE ASSOCIATION OR DEROZIANS

To spread their ideas, aims and objectives, the students or Derozians had been published following periodicals and journals from 1828 to 1844.

1. **The Parthenon**: In 1830 only one issue was published. After that it was discontinued.[20]
2. **Jnanannesan**: It means quest of knowledge. The journal was started in 1831 and continued up to 1844. With the active initiative of Rashik Krishna Mallick the journal had last long aimed to educate the people in scientific knowledge. The Christian Missionaries had also played an important part in support of the publication of Jnanannesan.[21] The journal propagated the new philosophy of Young Bengal and specially made some suggestions for the improvement of colonial administration and eradication of some social evils. Rashik

Krishna Mallick demanded the abolition of political power of the East India Company and the establishment of full parliamentary democracy. He also criticised the rampant corruption in the police force and demanded its remedies.[22]

3. **Enquirer**: It was started by Krishna Mohan Bandyopadhyay in 1831. The journal highly criticised the orthodox ideas of the then Hindu community as because they were always against the young radicals.[23]

4. **Hindu Pioneer**: The journal was started in 1838. It showed the social and political consciousness among the members of academic association or the Derozians. It published several articles on 'India and Foreigners' which complained of the people's exclusion from any share of the government and inexcusable burden of taxes.[24]

5. **The Quill**: It was started by Tarachand Chakraborty in 1834 aimed to criticise the policy of the government. He pointed out the unprotected status of the peasantry under the Permanent Settlement introduced by Lord Cornwallis in 1793. He strongly advocated the abolition of the political power of the merchant company.[25]

6. **Hesperus**: It was also a journal of Derozians aimed to publish articles criticising the superstition of the then orthodox Hindu society.[26]

7. **The Bengal Spectator**: Most probably, it was the last journal published by the Derozians. It was a monthly journal starting publication in 1842, but later on it became daily. Its main objective was to public the social, economic and political problems of the period. The Bengal Spectator began to agitate for competitive civil service examination.[27] The journal also published the articles favouring female education and widow remarriage question.

8. **The East Indian**: The journal was started by Derozio himself with the assistance of his students and continued till his death.[28]

9. **Athenium:** It was a monthly journal started by Madhav Chandra Mallick, member of Academic Association aimed to propagate their views in public.[29]

Impact

It can be kept in mind that from the beginning of the twentieth century and before the starting of organized student movement, the students moved unorganized way by writing against the irregularities, bondage and conservative attitude of British ruling. It was also observed that such student agitation against the British administration was initiated at Bengal first. The cause of such movement was to some extent for Bengal Renaissance. After Derozio the Academic Association did not stop their activities. They were alive till about 1839. David hare accepted the presidentship after Derozio. It was supplemented by an Epistolary Association in which the Derozians exchanged opinions in the true renaissance humanist style. It left a deep impact on the contemporary social and cultural organization. For instances, in 1838, on 12th March, with a view to form a permanent organization to discuss about different problems and crisis of the country, Tarinicharan Banerjee, Ramtanu Lahiri, Tarachand Chakraborty, Ramkrishna Dey, Ramgopal Ghosh and many others convened a meeting at Sanskrit College in Calcutta. Out of 200 participants who remained present in the meeting, most of them were the students, particularly the students from Hindu College. The outcome of the meeting was the formation of Society for the Acquisition of General Knowledge (1838). Its president was Tarachand Chakraborty, Vice president Ramgopal Ghose and Peary Chand Mitra was the first secretary. The society published three volumes of selection of papers presented at its meetings between 1840 and 1843. It was an intellectual organization which began to take shape as an anti-British sentiment. Their main agenda of discussion was civil and social reforms among Indians.[30] In 1841, the students and youths progressed one step more and they formed a half-shaped or, partial political platform or, organization in the name of "Deshhitaishi Sabha". The chief exponent of this Sabha was Sarada Prasad, an ex-student of Hindu College. It was declared that the Sabha or, organization was made for all the Indians irrespective of caste, creed or religion. "The objective of this newly made platform was stating the reasons that as the British rulers never allowed any political freedom to the Indians and they deprived of their right, which was the main cause behind the crisis and miseries of Indian people. So to get rid of this situation, Indians have to be united first to arrange to get relief from such torture and improper administration, the formation behind such unity would be the patriotism or, love for the country and the said platform or, organization would be run on the basis of welfare to the nation and its people in general."[31]The Derozian societies were youth cultural associations but they were being drawn towards politics.

The Academic Association did not last long because it failed to gather mass support from the Bengali society as well as intelligentsia. Even, Raja Rammohan Roy, the architect of renaissance Bengal did not support them. The contemporary society was dazed beyond measure by the activities of the Derozians, and yet they formed more of a group with a certain viewpoint than a real sustained movement with a solid basis and growing support. Being a group of brightest student of the country they created sensation and stir, but they failed to develop a definite progressing ideology. Their ideology was shaky. Therefore, they did not succeed to develop any movement outside their charmed circle. Practically, western type radical politics were hardly possible in Bengal at that time. Contemporary Bengali society was not prepared to expedite the radical movements. Apart from all these, the Derozians or the radical students attracted much attention for several years.

To sum up it can be said that few student organizations

were emerged in the period in scattering way, but academic association was the well organized student wing under the leadership of Derozio, a strangest figure in the history of Bengal Renaissance. The members and followers of the association were conscious both socially and politically. If it was not well organized, the association was failed to continue their activities after the death of Derozio. Even, the British rulers get alarmed and think how to tackle this rising dangerous trend!

HINDU MELA

The student society of Bengal gradually started to feel humiliation and bondage with the expansion of western education. The progress of path finding efforts were marked when Nabagopal Mitra and Rajnarayan Bose took a forward action to arrange a Hindu Mela in 1876 in Calcutta. At that time Jyotirindranath Tagore was a youth and he mentioned in his reminiscence that during that period Patriotic Songs, Poetry, Drama had influenced the student society deeply. The students of different schools and colleges murmured the songs of Rangalal Bandyopadhyay:

> "Swadhinata Hinotai Ke Banchite Chai Hae, Ke Banchite Chai
> Dasatta Srinkhal Bal Ke Paribe Pai Hae, ke Paribe Pai"
>
> (In Bengali)
>
> In bondage and humiliation, who could live?
> Who would chain his leg for slavery and dependency?
>
> (English Translation)
>
> Another Poet Michel Madhusudan Dutta's Song like:
> 'Rekha Maa Dashere Mone, A Minati Kori Pade"
>
> (In Bengali)
>
> Keep my mother in your mind, I do request on your leg
>
> (English Translation)

INDIAN ASSOCIATION

In 1876, the Indian Association was founded by Surendranath Banerjee, Anandamohan Bose and others. At least 7percent students remained present in the foundation ceremony or, first meeting of the Indian Association. Bipin Chandra Pal in his famous book entitled "Nabojuger Bangla" wrote "as Surendranath shaped the upcoming Bengali society with the help of students of Calcutta during that time, on the other hand the student society of that time helped to build leadership of Surendranath and Anandamohan in exchange of that contribution". In 1783, the students of Calcutta unitedly displayed their agitation against the Ilbert Bill. For showing dishonour to the court, the chief leader of this movement Surendranath was declared for imprisonment for which the student society expressed strong reaction and agitation against such verdict.[32] Not only in Calcutta, almost all schools and colleges of Bengal, students were involved in agitation by showing rally, arranging meeting, even they took part in strike also.

In this way, the consciousness for national interest and sentiment for a common effort started to bloom in the 19th century India which takes a shape for national movement in due course day by day. Afterwards, with the advent of national movement at the beginning of 20th century, the mass student agitation converted into a national movement.

STUDENT MOVEMENT IN THE TWENTIETH CENTURY (1902-1947)

Large sections of the society believe that the student movement began in the 20th century in India. But this conception is incorrect. The activities of the students' in the 19th and 20th centuries have been hardly highlighted by the scholars or, historians. The student community played a glorious role in the history of India through their memorable struggle and contributions .

The first two decades of the 20th century was full of students' movement. A huge number of Students' Associations were emerged in those two decades. At the beginning of the 20th century, we found the name of Dawn Society. It was very powerful student organization and purely non-political institute of culture, founded in 1902. The main spirit of the Dawn Society was Satish Chandra Mukherjee, a famous educationist and the editor of The Dawn, founded in 1897, which dealt with moral and spiritual ideas. He was assisted by Gurudas Banerjee, N. N. Ghosh, Sister Nivedita etc. It was formed mainly against the Indian Universities Commission and its unpopular report. The students thought that the report of the Universities Commission sought to destroy their identity, as well as educational system. A good number of educationists and students participated in the Dawn Society.[33] They demanded that the educational structure of India must be changed. They also advocated the bases of Swadeshi educational institutions which became an important part of the Swadeshi and anti-partition movement.

Another important objective of the Dawn Society was to teach moral and religious education to the students and to make them self-reliant. In 1903, they opened a Swadeshi Store to sell the home made goods. It was managed totally by the young students in the afternoon. The mouthpiece of the Dawn Society was The Dawn, regularly published the notes and news on the Indian economy. It proved that the swadeshi activities of the Dawn Society began much before the formal movement of 1905. After the announcement of partition of Bengal, the Dawn Society convened a meeting in which Satish Chandra Mukherjee, Rabindranath Tagore and Hirendranath Datta were present. Satish Chandra urged the students to sever connection with the official university and boycott its exams. They demanded the immediate establishment of a National University to promote national education.[34]

PARTITION OF BENGAL AND THE STUDENTS

One of the most unpopular and terrible measure of the British Indian Government was the Partition of Bengal in 1905. Lord Curzon came to India (1899-1905) with a strong determination to curtail the rising tide of nationalism. The Calcutta Corporation Act (1899), The Indian Universities Act (1904) and the Official Secrets Act (1904) were some of the measures through which Curzon sought to curb the growing nationalistic and patriotic spirit. One of the main objects of the partition of Bengal was to break up the unity of the people of Bengal. Lord Curzon divided the territories of Bengal in such a way that the western part of Bengal including Bihar, Chota Nagpur and Orissa formed the Hindu majority and the eastern part of Bengal including North Bengal and Assam formed the Muslim majority area. The plan of partition announced in newspapers on 20th July 1905, and finally became operational on 16th October 1905. The partition of Bengal produced tremendous anti-British reaction among the Bengalis. The partition of Bengal and subsequent swadeshi movement opened a new episode in the history of freedom movement of India. Though the movement started in Bengal it spread all over India. Starting from Bengal the agitation spread like wild fire in cities, towns and even villages where housewives, students and people of every corner in life participated to protest against the divisive policy of the Raj with zeal quite unprecedented in Indian history. A remarkable aspect of the movement was the widespread student participation all over Bengal, and in several other parts of India.[35] The students showed the greatest enthusiasm and created swadeshi spirit in Bengal and also India during the agitation.

ANTI-CIRCULAR SOCIETY

In July, 1905, the plan of partition had been opposed through an intensive use of the conventional moderate methods of press campaign, numerous meetings and petitions. The student community threw itself into the movements. A big Conference was held in the Town Hall of Calcutta in which the delegates of the students were spectacular. It was evident that total failure of such techniques led to a search for new way i.e. the boycott of British goods. They led the movement by holding pickets before the shops selling foreign goods and burning foreign clothes. In fact, never before had the students of Bengal been involved in such movement. Schools and college students in batches boycotted their classes to devote themselves to swadeshi activities. As expected, the British Indian Government took repressive measure to suppress the movement. The Government was terribly anxious at the student movement and so was forced to issue the infamous Carlyle Circular in order to put down the movement. It was named after the officiating chief secretary to the Government of Bengal R. W. Carlyle and was issued on 10th October 1905. The Circular prohibited the students from attending the meetings of the nationalist leaders or from boycotting, picketing or other activities associated with the swadeshi movement.[36] Even, shouting Vande Mataram was banned. The Carlyle Circular also threatening withdrawal of grants, scholarships and affiliation from nationalist dominated institutions led to a movement for boycott of official educational institutions and organizations of national schools which received a great incentive from the impressive donation of rupees one lac by Subodh Mullick.[37] The publication of Carlyle Circular created sensation and a sense of shock all over the country. As a protest against the notorious circular, a vast student meeting was convened at College Square on 4th November 1905, Calcutta and the outcome of the meeting was the formation of Anti-Circular Society under the leadership of Sachindranath Basu and Ramakanta Roy.[38]

After the formation of Anti-Circular Society, the students

undertook fund collection, campaigns for swadeshi goods and for national educational institutions under the banner of the society. The members of the society also arranged for continuance of the studies of those students who were victimized by the authorities.[3939] Krishna Kumar Mitra and his newspaper Sanjivini supported the students. They also popularized the national songs. In support of the Anti-Circular Society, Satish Chandra Mukherjee and his Dawn Society stepped forward. The Calcutta University was regarded as 'Goldighir Golam Khana'. The Anti-Circular Society had opened 75 Certres for selling swadeshi clothes and within 11 months more than one lakh rupees were earned by selling clothes.[40] The students hawked clothes from door to door.

It was very significant that during the swadeshi and boycott movement, the student volunteers of the Anti-Circular Society projected a National Flag of their own and handed over it to Surendranath Banerjee and his associates. In that projected flag, there was a tri coloured base- Red, Green and Yellow; in the middle of the flag, the students sketched eight half-bloom lotuses which marked as a symbol of the then eight provinces of India. They also sketched the sun and half moon on the flag to symbolize Hindu-Muslim unity.[41] In the middle was written in Devangiri script: Vande Mataram.[42]

The Anti-Circular Society was the mass student base organization. Its activities were spread to Dhaka, Naokhali, Mymansingh, Barisal, Jessore, Medinipur, Bankura and many other places. At this time the national consciousness of the students began to take shape.[43] The leaders of the society went to Jessore in February 1906, to restore communal harmony because there was a danger of riots in the place. In the Annual Report of the Society in 1906, Sachindranath Basu appealed the students to work for Hindu-Muslim unity. In the month of April 1906, at the Barisal Conference under the chairmanship of Abdul Rasul, the Anti-Circular Society defied ban on Vande

Mataram boldly. After that Sachindranath Basu and his associates were beaten by the British police and one of them was almost beaten to death, but he kept on shouting Vande Mataram.[44]It is to be noted that the activities of the apolitical students during that period was astonished the people. From the period 1905 to 1908, the movements of the students got its highest height and expectedly the Colonial Government brutally attacked the student leaders and even a number of students imprisoned in jails.[45]

Such a perspective of slow and unostentatious development of what Rabindranath called Atmasakti or self-strengthening had little appeal to the excited educated youth of Bengal. In another field, a considerable variety may be noticed within the national education efforts in Swadeshi Bengal, ranging from pleas for more technical training, through advocacy of vernacular medium.[46] After a couple of years the Bengal National College and a Bengal Technical Institute was set up. It was evident that a dozen of national schools in Bengal were also set up to spread the vernacular education.

NATURE OF THE MOVEMENT

There was a great debate among the scholars about the student participation in the anti-partition or swadeshi and boycott movement. The character and trend of this movement were different from all previous movements of the 19th century. So from the stand point of achievement its importance could not be judged. A section of scholars had opined that the Muslim students did not show their solidarity to the movements. Dr. Hannan, a noted Bangladeshi historian said the middle class Muslims of East Bengal supported the partition of Bengal on the ground that Dhaka was announced as their new capital. But a number of Muslim politician and student leaders involved in the anti-partition movement and even took the leading role. Muslim Student leaders like Abdul Rasul, Abdul Halim

Gajnavi, Moniruzzaman Islamabadi, Moulabi Kazim Ali, Syed Ismail Hossain Siraji, Abul Qasim, Mujibur Rahaman, Moulana Akram Khan, Dr. Abdul Gaffur Siddhiki, Syed Ali Imam, Hassan Imam, Mojarul Hoque, Liyakat Hussain were prominent. These Muslim student leaders were participated in the anti-partition movement with full strength and showed solidarity to the nationalist leaders of the movement.[47]

One of the most important characteristics of the movement was the active participation of the Hindu and Muslim zamindars of East Bengal. They apprehended that their zamindary system may be abolished on the ground of partition. The ordinary people were agonized and frustrated with the inhuman attitude of the zamindars and exploitation by the zamindary system.[48]Another peculiar characteristics of the student participation in the anti-partition movement was that the students of mofussil area either reluctant or non-interested. The contemporary Newspapers and Periodicals do not provide us any information of the mofussil students on anti-partition movement. During 1905-1908 Bengal mofussil students was not prepared to expedite their solidarity on the issue of the partition.

During the anti-partition movement many items like ink, nibs and matches were produced locally and the students used these swadeshi goods. Much student involvement in the movement also attracted the attention of the British Parliament. In a parliamentary session, dealing with the educational institutions of Government prosecutions against students, Dr. Ratherford asked the Secretary of State for India whether his attention had been drawn to occurrences of such cases or not.[49]

Impact

The student participation and their active involvement in the anti-partition or swadeshi and boycott movement had left a deep impact in a number of ways. Its impact was felt at every stage in the life of Bengal and also of India in the arena of literature, music, art, science and education. The patriotism, sacrifice and courage of the students earned great respect from the common people. Influence of the student movements have been perhaps most pronounced in the literary and cultural life of the state. In literature, writers and poets have introduced a new tone and outlook.[50] The agitating students habitually recite their poems in the various meetings and demonstrations. In the public meetings, rallies and demonstrations the agitating students staged dramas, which helped to create a new outlook. In addition to these, the students brought out many leaflets, booklets, Chharas or rhymes which also influenced the common masses of Bengal. The famous song of Rabindranath Tagore 'Banglar Mati, Banglar Jal' i.e. soil and climate of Bengal was composed in the light of swadeshi movement. On the other hand, political leaflets were extensively circulated amongst the students. Political songs of Bankim Chandra Chattopadhyay's Anandamath were memorized by the students. The students were also used to held exhibition where paintings of Lala Lajpat Rai, Aurobindo Ghosh, Bipin Chandra Pal were displayed.[51] The agitating students spread the anti-partition movement from Bengal to other parts of the country especially South India. Bipin Chandra Pal took the leading role to spread the movement in south. In 1907, He visited Vizagapatnam, Madras, Rajahmundhry etc. for delivering lectures on the movement and got a tremendous response from the students of south. Even the student of Madras bears the expenses of his visit.[52]

Ultimately, the British Indian Government bowed down to public opinion and repealed the Partition Act in 1911.But there was no restoration of the former condition of Bengal and marked as the most unfortunate tragedy in the history of Bengal. It heralded the path of success for any future upheaval.

After swadeshi movement, several students' organizations were coming up. With the active initiative of Surendranath

Banerjee, a new Students' Association namely Brotherhood was formed in 1914 in Calcutta. Netaji Subhash Chandra Bose and Prafulla Chandra Ghosh was the active member of this association.[53] Their goal was to spread the nationalist activities in the different parts of Bengal.

The proposal for launching the Non-Cooperation movement was accepted in the Nagpur Session of the Indian National Congress in 1920. This was first ever all India agitation concerning liberation of the country led by Gandhiji in 1921. This movement got a tremendous response from the student community of Bengal. Thousands of students left their schools and colleges shouting Gandhiji Ki Jai and Bandemataram. A section of students from City College, Vidyasagar College and Ripon College of Calcutta left their study and joined the movement. On 20th January, 1921, a student strike was held at Calcutta and vowed not to return to college till independence was achieved.[54] They also protested with black flag during the visit of Crown-Prince at Calcutta. On 25th December, 1920, the All India College Students Conference (AICSC) was held at Nagpur under the chairmanship of Lala Lajpat Rai. In this Conference a Resolution was adopted for establishing national colleges for the students. It was the first all India conference of the students in this country. The news of the formation of the AICSC spread like wildfire all over country. It played an important part in raising their consciousness. In this movement so many students were arrested and punished by the British repressive machinery.[55]

In November, 1927, the then British Prime Minister Baldwin surprised the Indian people by announcing the decision of the British Cabinet to constitute the Simon Commission for preempting any possibility of taking any favourable reform measure in India. What shocked the Indians was the decision to exclude Indian member from the body which was to prepare the future constitution of India. On 3rd February, 1928, when the Commission arrived in India, there was a nationwide hartal (strike) observed. Huge procession marched the streets of different parts of our country. Middle class students and youths dominated such urban demonstrations. From 1928 to 1929, there were full of students' and youths' conferences and associations. The youths and students demanded complete independence and radical social and economic changes. Educated unemployment may have had something to do with this wave of youth unrest.[56] Most of schools and colleges observed hartal in Calcutta also. It was for the first time a section of female students from Bethune College of Calcutta joined the strike against Simon Commission. The students of Presidency College staged dharna in front of the college under the leadership of Promod Kumar Ghosal, the then General Secretary of the Students' Union of the Presidency College. During this protest movement the police took a repressive measure by using force on the protesting students. Promod Kumar Ghosal was injured seriously in this police atrocity. Immediately after this incident, thousands of students assembled at College Square, Calcutta, to protest against this brutal attack of the British police. The police also used same tactics in other colleges who were protesting against Simon Commission. After these severe incidents, there was a need for a united student association. To this a resolution was adopted in the meeting of all Bengal students held on 17th February, 1928, in the Albert Hall of Calcutta under the chairmanship of Prof. Nripen Chandra Bandyopadhyay. In this meeting Promod Kumar Ghosal, Birendranath Dasgupta and Amarendranath Roy took a leading role. About 500 students from different districts of Bengal were attended the conference. The outcome of the conference was the birth of All Bengal Students' Association (ABSA) on 23rd September, 1928. Its main aim was to form vernacular group of the students, establishing night schools for the workers etc. With the beginning of ABSA, the self-strengthening student movement began in Bengal.[57] But soon ABSA was divided into two groups- ABSA and BPSA on ideological grounds.

The deferment of the Civil Disobedience Movement and the situation after that, the influence of the ideas of Bhagat Singh and his associates propagated widely through their point of view in the court, their consequent martyrdom, the influence of the developments taking place at the global level i.e. quick progress of the USSR through planned economy, anti-colonial movements throughout the world etc. contributed to the creation of various organizations to mobilize different sections of the society in the freedom struggle.[58] From 1933 onwards the nature of student movement quieted down for some time. The wave started after 1935, because there was an active effort to unite all students' organizations under one national umbrella. In 1936, the All India Students' Federation (AISF) was created in Lucknow at the All India Students Convention. Md. Ali Zinnah presided over the Convention, and it was inaugurated by Pandit Jawaharlal Nehru. In this convention, Md. Zinnah and Pandit Nehru encouraged the students for building up strong organization irrespective of caste and class. Pandit Nehru had appealed the students to view the Indian struggle for independence as a part of the struggle against colonialism taking place across the world. Nehru had distinctively brought the Palestinian liberation struggle and the fight against fascism in Spain to the notice of the conference. The development and understanding of the student movement organizers of those times, their intense observation of the international developments can be understood from another resolution that the conference accepted on the growth of fascist forces. The AISF had a pro-independence and radical mission and alert on independence for India from British rule. This focus initially helped association the various basics of the Indian student organization and drew on popular support for the independence cause among students.[59] The main aims and objectives of the AISF were as follows:

1. to encourage cultural and intellectual cooperation on equal terms between the students of various provinces and Indian states, and between students of India and other parts of the world.
2. to suggest improvements in the present educational systems
3. to safeguard the rights of the student community and
4. to prepare the students for citizenship in order to take their due share in the struggle for complete national freedom by arousing their social, political and economic consciousness.

The conference also decided to start an official organ, The Students' Tribune, to propagate its views.[60]

1. Ventilate the grievances of the students to support their cause and organize them into a powerful organization.
2. Seek to solve the problem of unemployment
3. Inculcate the spirit of simple living and high thinking
4. Agitate against the rate system of education

All these show that the pioneers of Indian student movement never visualized the student movement as a strand by itself and disconnect from the concerns of the society at large. They sought to assimilate the students in the national movement by organizing them first on the issues that are of direct concern to them and then gradually developing their political consciousness. They were driven by an unconquerable urge to free the country from all kinds of restraints and not just the foreign rule.[61]

The ideological and cultural differences within Indian society scattered the student organization soon. The burning example was the creation of the All-India Muslim Students

Federation (AIMSF) in 1937. The AIMSF's target was the formation of a separate Muslim state and they eventually contributed to the creation of Pakistan. The beginning of the World War II led to further division of the student movement. Within the AISF, tension rose between those students sustaining participation in the war effort (by and large leftist students supporting the decision of Soviet Russia to enter the war), and those students in opponent to joining the war (Socialists and Gandhian students). The ultimate result was the formation of the All-India Students Congress[62] (AISC) which became the unsurpassed student organization in the late 1940s bearing into Indian independence.

In 1945, a section of the students participated in the protest movements organised all over Bengal for the liberation of the prisoners of the Azad Hind Fauj. The British police took repressive measure to suppress the movement. In this police atrocities one student was killed namely Rameswar Mukherjee. This incident led to the violent student movement in Bengal. On 11th February, 1946 the police unleashed hostility on a demonstration demanding the release of Captain Rashid Ali of the Azad Hind Fauj organised jointly by the Students' Federation and Muslim Students' League. Again the people of all walks erupted in antagonism. The congress termed the people's impulsive protests 'hooliganism'.[63] From this time onward the Congress seemed cautious of the mass uprising gradually gaining momentum throughout India. In July the Surabardi Government of Bengal complied with the demands of students and the public to release political prisoners. In 1946, the students of Bengal also involved in support of Naval Mutiny. The Students' Federation along with the various organisations of the working class gave the uprising its full support. The Naval Mutiny had the potential of turning into a huge mass uprising. But the Congress and Muslim League withdrew support from the rebels. Prominent Congress leader

Sarder Patel remarked that Naval Mutiny is a kind of anarchy, it should stop right now. I am agreed with the Naval Chief that discipline should be maintained.[64]Students also participated in the Tebhaga Movement of Bengal against the exploitation of the zamindars. During those days more and more female students took part in the struggle.

There were various factors mentioned above that led down the penetration of the students' movement in the soil of West Bengal before independence. The students involved themselves with the various socio-economic movements. These contributed largely to strengthen the popular beliefs of the students.

Popularity of the student movement had accorded an unmistakable legitimacy in West Bengal. The reasons for this distinctive development are not far-flung to seek. Geo-politically, West Bengal stood far away from the seat of power save for the period of the British Raj during which Calcutta was the capital of India. In the field of culture and religion also Bengal maintained a distance from the Brahmonical heartland of India, for she never accepted the orthodox way of life as sanctioned by the Vedas. The Aryans scoffed at the people who visited Bengal. According to them, Bengal was inhibited by people of low origin.[65] For a long period, the influence of Aryan civilization was rather marginal on the Bengalee people, as the Bengalees had an aversion for Vedic rites and rituals. Bengalee people who mainly belong to the Austric race did not discard their old folkways and mores.[66] Rigorous caste system as sanctioned by the Vedas did not go deep into the Bengalee mind. By contrast, Buddhism which recognized no caste distinction and which upheld an ideal of equality had immediate appeal to the Bengalee people. The common people of Bengal, by accepting the Buddhist cult, expressed their opposition to orthodox Hinduism.

Thus, historically set apart from the currents of convention accepted by the rest of the country, Bengal always exhibited a spirit rational self-identity. A tendency to challenge what others never think twice to accept, a tendency to think ahead of others and a tendency to go on building and breaking the tradition represent. In short, it is the key to the social psychology and political temperament of Bengal. Bengal's sacrifice and sufferings in pre-independence days are known to all, but in post-independence period planned exclusion of Bengal from the benefits of nation building, rapid decline of its glorious city, influx of millions of refugees, growing economic gloom of the people have caused a sense of deprivation among the Bengalee people as also the students.[67] This is why the student movement which lay emphasis on the politics of protest enjoys a large following and support base in the state.

NOTES AND REFERENCES

1. Dasgupta, H. and Adhikary, H. (1993 & 2008): Rajnaitik Poto Bhumite Bharatiya Upamahadesher Chhatra Andolan (in Bengali), School for People, Medinipore, and Radical Impression, Kolkata, p. 365.
2. Sarkar, S. N. (1974): Student Unrest: A Socio-Psychological Study, Indian Book Exchange, Kolkata, p. 3.
3. Ibid.
4. Ibid.
5. Dasgupta, H. and Adhikary, H. (1993 & 2008), p. 366.
6. Rajimwale, Anil (2001): History of Student Movement in India; Origins and Development (1920-1947), Manak Publications Pvt. Ltd., New Delhi, pp. 2-3.
7. Rashid, Ali Syed (1997): Culture of Student Politics, Inter-India Publications, New Delhi, pp. 15-17.
8. Shah Ghanshyam (2004): Social Movements in India, Sage Publication Pvt. Ltd., New Delhi, pp. 105-107.
9. Dasgupta, H. and Adhikary, H. (1993 & 2008), p. 366.
10. Rajimwale, Anil (2001): op. cit. pp. 1-3.

11. Khai Thrombosis: *Bharatkosa (1967)* (in Bengali), Vol. III, *Bangiya Sahitya Parisad,* Kolkata, p. 409.
12. Sarkar, Susobhan (1970): Bengal Renaissance and Other Essays, People's Publishing House, New Delhi, p. 11.
13. Rajimwale, Anil (2001): op. cit., p. 7.
14. Ibid.
15. Dasgupta, Hiren and Adhikary Harinarayan (1993 & 2008): op. cit., pp. 16-17.
16. History and General Studies (2015), retrieved from www.selfstudyhistory.com, pp. 1-3.
17. Bhattacharya Bhavani (1980): Socio-Political Currents in Bengal: A Nineteenth Century Perspective, Vikas Publishing House Pvt. Ltd., New Delhi, p. 4.
18. Rajimwale, Anil (2001): op. cit. pp. 8-9.
19. Sarkar, Susobhan (1979): On the Bengal Renaissance, Papyrus, Kolkata, pp. 28-29.
20. Banglapedia (updated version, 2014): National Encyclopaedia of Bangladesh, retrieved from http://en.banglapaedia.org
21. Ibid.
22. Sarkar, Susobhan (1979): op. cit., p. 107-108.
23. *Banglapedia (2014)*: Ibid.
24. Sarkar Susobhan (1979): op. cit., p. 107-108.
25. Ibid.
26. *Banglapedia (2014)*: Ibid.
27. Sarkar, Susobhan (1979): op. cit., p. 107-108.
28. Banerjee, Tarashankar (1972): "The Young Bengal: A General Estimate" in Renascent Bengal (1817-1857), Calcutta, p. 58
29. Sarkar, Susobhan (1979): op. cit., p. 106-108.
30. Rajimwale, Anil (2001): op. cit. p. 10.
31. Calcutta Monthly Journal (1981), November Issue, pp. 3-5.
32. Khai, T. (1967), p. 409.
33. Rajimwale, Anil: History of Student Movement in India: Origins

and Development (1920-1947), Manak Publications Pvt. Ltd., New Delhi, 2001, p.44.

34. Majumdar, Ramesh Chandra: History of the Freedom Movement in India, Vol. II, Firma K. L. M., Calcutta, 1963, pp.75-76.
35. Rajimwale, Anil: History of Student Movement in India: Origins and Development (1920-1947), Manak Publications Pvt. Ltd., New Delhi, 2001, p.44.
36. Majumdar, R. C.: op. cit. p. 62.
37. Sarkar, Sumit: Modern India: 1885-1947, Macmillan, New Delhi, 1983, pp. 111-112.
38. Chattopadhyay, Gautam: Bengal's Student Movement in Challenge: A Saga of India's Struggle for Freedom, People's Publishing House, New Delhi, 1984, p. 515.
39. Rajimwale, Anil: op. cit. p. 47.
40. Chattopadhyay Gautam: op. cit. p. 516.
41. Dasgupta, H. and Adhikary, H.: Rajnaitik Poto Bhumite Bharatiya Upamahadesher Chhatra Andolan (in Bengali), School for People, Medinipore, 1993, and Radical Impression, Kolkata, 2008, pp. 25-26.
42. Chattopadhyay, Gautam: op. cit. p. 516.
43. Rajimwale, Anil: op. cit., p.44.
44. Chattopadhyay, Gautam: op. cit. p. 516.45 . Mohammed Hannan: History of Student Movement of Bangladesh; 1830-1971, Osman Goni Agamee Prakashani, Dhaka, Bangladesh, 1999, p. 32.
46. Sarkar, S.: Modern India: 1885-1947, Macmillan, 1983, p. 112 and also see The Swadeshi Movement in Bengal.
47. Mohammed Hannan: op. cit. p. 30.
48. Ibid.
49. Rajimwale, Anil: op. cit. p. 47.
50. Ray, Sudhir: Marxist Parties of West Bengal: 1947-2001, Progressive Publisher, Kolkata, 2001, pp. 253-255.

51. Rajimwale, Anil: op. cit. p. 49.
52. V. Sankaran Nair: Swadeshi Movement; The Beginnings of Student Unrest in South India, Mittal Publications, Delhi, 1985, pp. 43-45.
53. Khai, T. (1967): Bharatkosa (in Bengali), Vol. III, Bangiya Sahitya Parisad, Kolkata, pp. 409-410.
54. The History of the SFI and the Students' Movement in India, www.sfiwb.org
55. Khai, T. (1967), p. 409.
56. Sarkar, S.(1983), p. 266.
57. Khai, T. (1967), pp.410-411.
58. People's Democracy, Vol. XXX, No. 36, Sep. 03, 2006, R. Arun Kumar's Article on '*Seventy Years of Organized Student Movement*'.
59. People's Democracy, Vol. XXX, No. 36, Sep. 03, 2006.
60. Dasgupta, H. and Adhikary, H.(1993 & 2008), p. 100.
61. People's Democracy, Vol. XXX, No. 36, Sep. 03, 2006.
62. Khai, T.(1967), p. 412.
63. The History of the SFI and the Students' Movement in India, www.sfiwb.org
64. Amrita Bazar Patrika, 25.02.1946.
65. "It is evident that even in the later Brahmonical literature the primitive tribes of Bengal were regarded as dasyus or transgressors by the sages", History of Bengal, First Edition, The University of Dacca, 1943, p. 35.
66. "We may therefore legitimately draw the inference that the primitive peoples of Bengal were different in race and culture, and perhaps in both, from the Aryans who compiled the Vedic Literature", History of Bengal, First Edition, The University of Dacca, 1943, p. 35.
67. Ray, S. (2007): Marxist Parties of West Bengal: 1947-2001, Progressive, Kolkata, p. 35.

3

Role of Students in Popular Protest Movements of Bengal (1947-1956)

The movement launched by the students of Bengal against the British imperialism was continued after the declaration of Independence of India. But the nature of the students' movement was altered after Independence. In this period their movement was against the unpopular activities of the independent Government but in favour of socio-economic improvement of the country. The proposal of the partition of the country raised by Lord Mountbatten evoked a sort of protest or rather upsurge of the student community of Bengal. They proposed that the Hindus and Muslims of Bengal should linger in India with their own religious beliefs. But the fact cannot be denied that the students standing on the threshold of independence could not refrain outside the realm of political turmoil of the time. In reality, the student community was in the vortex of the political circumstances of the time. The students could not keep themselves off from the political fend that rocked the political firmament of the time.[1] Ultimately India achieved Independence at the mid night of 14th August, 1947. Immediately, after the proclamation of Independence, the Indian subcontinent was divided into two parts— India and Pakistan. After Independence, there occurred a sort of change in the characteristics of the students' movement of the different students' organization.

After passing Indian Independence Act India became an

'Independent Union' w.e.f. the midnight of 14th August, 1947. Lord Mountbatten, the then Viceroy of India transferred power to the hand of the Indian Parliament. Similarly Power was also transferred to the Pakistan Dominion. Pandit Jawaharlal Nehru, the First Prime Minister of Free India, in a historic speech before the Indian Parliament, on the midnight of 14th August said "On August 15, in a historic ceremony, the Indian Tri Colour Flag was raised at the Red Fort at Delhi replacing the Union Jack. India started on a new course of her history after the dawn of her independence."[2]

The people of India, by and large, expected that freedom would beget food, dress and rehabilitation for them. They further aspired that freedom would be the source of illumination of the people through light of education and it would ensure opportunity for employment. The leaders of Indian freedom movement promised accordingly to the people at large before independence. They promised to develop India in a manner that would redeem the expectation of the people. They put before the people the image of Golden India. They also assured to build India in the manner where there would be no room for exploitation and black marketers. Even Pandit Nehru threatened to bash them in commendable manner. In reality, what they did practically differed from what the pledged to do. Simultaneously, with the independence there cropped a series of socio-economic problems such as the problem of refugee influx, food crisis, employment crisis, housing crisis etc.[3] The problem may be studied from another point of view. The modern sector of the economy in West Bengal is heavily dominated by Non-Bengalees. As a consequence, parts of the earnings are exported. Since expectation has been rising faster than economic output, it is not unreasonable to suppose that the degree of relative deprivation experienced by people living in West Bengal, Bihar and U.P. must be quite high. If this is true, a large magnitude of political unrest in these states can also be expected.[4] Naturally unemployment problem, especially problem of educated unemployment has assumed an alarming proportion in West Bengal. This has caused wide-spread discontent among the youths and the students. A considerable section of the youth has not only lost faith in the Congress, but also in parliamentary politics. Critics opine that parliamentary leftists have failed to provide leadership to the rural landless and the urban youths, weighed down as they are with constitutional obligations and bogged down in electoral politics.[5] The student community of Bengal failed to keep themselves away from those problems. They also rallied round the movement.

Immediately, after independence, the Congress Party announced that the students should not mingled with politics, students should plunged themselves into studies for the development of the country. So, there was no need to constitute students' organization. Showing instance immediately, the Congress Party jumbled their students' organization. The other political parties failed to get on with the attitude of the Congress Party. Weiner remarked that "Eager to push students out of politics and into development work, Congress lost ground to the opposition parties, who in the meantime were winning student participation for electioneering work against the government and support for various movements against existing authorities."The question of the crippling of the students' organization could not dent them seriously. The fundamental difference between the students' movement in pre-independence and that of the post-independence became obvious. Firstly, no students' organization had any independent entity in the post-independence period. They became completely engrossed with political parties of their linking. Only the AISF affiliated to Communist Party of India dilate its influence throughout the country. It was only in West Bengal all the political parties gave birth to students' organization of their own such as Chhatra Bloc affiliated to Forward Bloc, Progressive Students' Union affiliated to Revolutionary Socialist Party, Democratic Students' Organization affiliated to Socialist Unity Centre of India, and Students' Association affiliated to Socialist Party etc. Even the Congress Party brought into being Chhatra Parisad as their students' wing in Bengal.[6] Meanwhile, the disappearance of the Communal Student League affiliated to Muslim League and pampering of the secessionist movement by the Hindu Communalist or, Hindu Chauvinists extended lengthening shadow of impending danger in the students' movement in Bengal.[7]

CHANGING CHARACTERISTICS OF MOVEMENTS

In the Post-Independence era, there was a marked change of perspective of the student movements. It remains unabated and in many cases the movements have assumed alarming aspect. The goals of the different movements of the students, fighting in different political banners are not only political, but also social, economic, humanistic and cultural. The students of all countries have always swooped down upon with constructive mind for the development of their countries. They have embarked upon the reconstruction like unrestricted waves and have rocked seriously upon the existing political, social, economic and cultural structures.[8] The students involved in the movements irrespective of caste, colour and creed. The movements of the students of West Bengal are no exceptions to that. The character of the movements of the students of West Bengal began changing since 1960s. Starting as nationalists they gradually assumed left and extreme ideology. In the place of the mass student organizations, a number of local groups mostly of an informal nature have developed.

An immense expansion of the Indian higher education system following independence also had a significant impact on the development of the student movement in India. In the

1960s increase of institutions and enrolment resulted in a larger number of university graduates. Consequently, significant numbers of university graduates found underemployment or unemployment as they left the university. This situation was a harsh contrast from the guarantees of civil service or professional positions experienced by previous generations of students. At that time the University Grants Commission reported to the Union Government of India regarding students' movement in the various universities of India. The Report points out:

"In India students have come to regard the Students Union merely as a bargaining counter or as a forum for voicing their 'grievances'. In fact the Unions have become a peculiar type of Trade Union. Like Trade Unions, the office bearers negotiate with the University Authorities on behalf of the students. It has also been found that political parties take an active interest in the Students' Union elections and in many Universities and Colleges the election are fought on party basis as directed by the existing political parties. Usually, office bearers of the Unions are senior students who have been in the University for 4 to 5 years; but in certain Universities, there are some union leaders who have stayed in the University for 8 to 9 years or even for a much longer period. Such 'professional' student leaders are often responsible for misguiding the fresh entrants to our Universities and they try to earn cheap popularity by championing 'the cause of the students' under trivial pretexts of such matters that are not the concern of the students at all."[9]

Pandit Jawaharlal Nehru too stated that "Another major reason for student unrest and fall in standards is the undue importance given to the final examination. Students are able to neglect their works throughout the year and cram in the last few months in order to pass and get a degree......our education at present is sometimes lacking in a moral or ethical tone. India is a secular state, but it does not imply any disregard for moral values. We have a very high spiritual heritage but the young generations are sometime insufficiently aware of this....”[10]

PARTICIPATION IN POPULAR PROTEST MOVEMENTS

After the attainment of Independence, the students involved in various socio-economic movements, or the popular protest movements, such as movement against the brutal murder of Gandhiji, movement in favour of the refugees, movement against the hike of Tram fare, Teachers’ movement, Anti-Merger movement of West Bengal and Bihar, Food movement which were an annual event, peasant movement, protest against National Emergency and so on. This chapter deals with the first five movements up to 1956 mentioned above.

MOVEMENT AGAINST THE MURDER OF GANDHIJI

“Gandhi was inevitable. If humanity is to progress, Gandhi is inescapable. He lived, thought and acted, inspired by the vision of humanity evolving toward a world of peace and harmony. We may ignore Gandhi at our own risk.”

— Dr. Martin Luther King Jr.

On the 30th January, 1948 Gandhi woke up at his usual hour, 3.30 am. After the Morning Prayer he did the final shapes to the new constitution for Congress which he had been unable to finish the last night. The rest of the morning was spent for answering letters. Someone mentioned the fact that despite his pitiable health, he was working relentlessly. He explained “Tomorrow I may not be here.” If I have to die, I should like to die at the prayer meeting. You are wrong in believing that you can protect me from impairment. God is my protector.[11] Then, while holding a prayer gathering at Birla House, Delhi, Gandhi was shot dead by Nathuram Godse. A nation’s father was died.

In reality, Gandhiji was assassinated by the extreme reactionary conspiracy of Vinayak Godse, Gopal Godse and many others. The whole of India was in the scourge of tremendous mourning immediately after the brutal murder of Gandhiji. Next day the people of all walks of life burst forth in anger and protest. The student community did not lag behind. In different parts of India, the students setting aside their party allegiance or affiliation and overthrowing the barriers of the schools and colleges congregated outside in protest. Their object was to protest vociferously against the brutal murder of the great man of India and simultaneously they condemned the ghastly shedding of blood by the Hindu communalists.[12]

After the assassination of Gandhi, Prime Minister Jawaharlal Nehru addressed the Nation through Radio:

"Friends and comrades, the light has gone out of our lives, and there is darkness everywhere, and I do not quite know what to tell you or how to say it. Our beloved leader, Bapu as we called him, 'the Father of the Nation', is no more. Perhaps I am wrong to say that; nevertheless, we will not see him again, as we have seen him for these many years, we will not run to him for advice or seek solace from him, and that is a terrible blow, not only for me, but for millions in this country."[13]

The purpose behind the participation of the students was to indoctrinate spirit of peace, love and brotherhood among the entire nation. The students of Bengal ensured their active involvement in the movement. Someplace, students were wearing clothes in Khadi to show their participation and eagerness to mark the Gandhian spirit of non-violence and truth. Students delivered speeches for highlighting Gandhi's philosophy.[14] Students further clued-up that he was a selfless leader and suffered many hardships for the independence of our country.

PARTICIPATION IN REFUGEE MOVEMENT

As a fall out of the partition of the country, millions of refugees migrated to the West Punjab from the East Punjab and vice versa. Similarly the refugees also migrated from East Bengal to West Bengal. The problem of Punjab was resolved by the then Congress Government of Delhi as very human manner and with realistic sensitivity. But in case of West Bengal the Congress Government of Delhi did not deal with the problem of the refugees with same revelation. In reality, the Union Government was reluctant to take responsibility for the rehabilitation of the refugees from East Bengal and as a result the Government exhibited utter inhuman attitude on that score.[15]

The history of the migration of the Hindus from East Pakistan after partition is one of the most terrible episodes of present-day history. It is the saga of the uprooting of a virile population exceedingly attached to their beautiful land. In Bengal, it was a heartbreaking prolonged process. It started before partition with the Naokhali riots of 1946 and continues downstairs to this day. The migrants came in an impression. At times the migration hit West Bengal in the shape of horrible breakers and often subsided into a trickle. But, except for a very brief time, it never stopped. It will not bring to an end until the last of the non-Muslims is driven out of that country. This is the approved manner of solving the minority trouble in Islamic countries. So the frustrating treks from the East to the West countries. In the meantime, East Pakistan has transformed itself into Bangladesh in 1971. But the process has not been kept back except for the lucid interval of the Mujib Regime. Gradually but steadily a whole people is being squeezed out of the country by economic and social exclusion and by pogroms at regular intervals.[16] The sense of uncertainty which developed among the East Bengal Hindus during the hatred campaign between the Nizam and the Government of India foregoing the police action led to an anxious migration from East

Pakistan.[17] The refugees who sought shelter in Government camps represented only a small division of the total influx. A huge number of those who crossed into West Bengal, Tripura and Assam tried to fend for themselves. The Census of 1951 was at least 3.5 million refugees in West Bengal.

As a result of the large scale influx of refugees, there cropped up the problems of food, dress and rehabilitation. On the other hand, the independent Government of India and the State Government of that time did not deal with the refugees in human manner and it led the refugees to rise in movement. The then opposition parties also stood by them. On 11th January, 1949 the refugees brought out procession from Sealdah Station, Calcutta to place their demands, but the police resorted random lathi charge and used tear gas to disperse the rebellious refugees in the street. On the next day i.e. 12th January, 1949 the students, as a mark of protest against the brutal act of the police, organized strike and supported the demands of the refugees. Thereafter, on 18th January, 1949 responding to the call of BPSF thousands of students assembled at the premises of Calcutta University. A meeting was held and they organized a protest rally. As expected, the police used force to disperse the protesting students. The agitating students also started to throw brick ball upon the police. The students set blazing the trams, buses etc. and erected barricades in the streets. In the police actions about six persons including four students were killed. Before that some refugees had to lose their lives in police firing in Delhi while the refugees were in procession to place their charter of demands to the Prime Minister. To protest against these incidents the students organized meetings and decided to launch movement against police atrocities. In the next day when the rebellious students went to the Morgue of Calcutta Medical College for bringing the bodies of dead students, killed in police firing, police action was took place there also and even firing in which five students were killed. Mr. Dilip Basu, the student leader of Charu Chandra College, Kolkata and many others were hospitalized after undergoing police firing. When they were in need of blood hundreds of students flocked before the Blood Bank of Calcutta Medical College to donate blood.[18]Thus, refugee movement was converted into a student movement with intensified thrust.

Some Communist leaders who came from East Bengal started association among the refugees. They insisted that refugees should be rehabilitated within west Bengal, before sending them somewhere else without making any prior preparations for their settlement. During the years 1948-1950, students often rupture into heated protests against police atrocities and terror. They demanded the release of the film entitled 'Forty Two', organized meetings, mass signature campaigns against precautionary detention, and sought to arouse public sympathy over mass hunger strikes and police firings in the prisons of west Bengal.[19] The College Street area of Calcutta repeatedly witnessed violent student demonstrations in those days.[20]

It is worthy of mention that the roughness between the students and the police stopped after the continuous fighting between them for four days at a stretch. The students failed to gain much for the refugees by dint of the students' movement.

After the formation of the United Central Refugee Council (UCRC), most of the problems of the refugees were removed. Leaders like Ambika Chakraborty, Abdul Halim, Anil Singha, Gopal Banerjee, Kamala Dasgupta etc. were prominent in this refugee movement. On the other hand, Sri Nripen Banerjee, Saroj Hazra, Kamal Chatterjee, Sukhendu Majumdar were the prominent student leader who led this movement in full swing. During this period, some of them arrested shortly. It can be said that gradually the refugee movement was transformed into a massive student movement and its main objective was to plunge into a confrontation with the police while it launched any rally on the avenues in Calcutta and the districts level. Observing the trend of students' movement on the road, the CPI in its Secret Manifesto described that such students' movement should be spread and converted into a 'Barricade Movement', which would be helped to create an environment of revolt in a greater sense everywhere. Henceforth, these students' movement was guided with this intension throughout the Bengal to reap the harvest at large.[21]

It was carefully marked that while the students' movement in support of the demands of the refugees was shifted mainly against the then Congress led Government, in response to that anti-government attitude, the Congress Government with its police and official machineries initiated more antagonistic and inhuman action to nip down students' agitation with strong handed attitude. To cope up with the situation created for the students' agitation, the then Police Commissioner of Calcutta openly declared that "to save lives of hundred people, it is better to take one life by firing".[22] In one side, the theory and objective to convert the students' movement into a clashing with the police in general and on the other side, the drastic action and efforts taken by police force and its authority, to resist such attacking activities by the students upon the police, as a result, in between the two opposite pressures, the common and mass students kept them apart from such movement and tussle.

MOVEMENT AGAINST THE HIKE OF TRAM FARE

In the early part of 1950s, the students came forward in support of the Calcutta Tramways workers, when the workers initiated strikes and agitation. But, an important point had been marked that such agitation of Tram workers could not reflect any impression or, created any influence upon any District as it was related only with the people of the then Calcutta jurisdiction; though at that time BPSF made a common target to transform all movements into an agitation against the then Congress Government.

The main reason of Tram Workers' movement was against the enhancement of Tram Fare. The Calcutta Tramways Company was a British-owned concern registered in London. Even after the transfer of power in 1947, British ownership sustained.[23] Immediately after the transfer of power in August 1947, the tram company was once more held with the idea of raising the fare. But this time people from all corners of life threatened not to pay the enhanced fares and to boycott trams.[24] On June 25, 1953 the company announced its decision to increase second class fares from the July 1, 1953. The Calcutta Tram Company raised its fare 1 paise by which this foreign company could earn a profit of Rs. 30 lakhs, in addition to its earning of Rs. 2.5 crore per annum. The decision was supported by the then Government of West Bengal. For this fare raising steps taken by CTC, people from all walks came on the road in protest of such decision of the CTC. The students in general also joined this movement. They not only expressed their compliance with this public sentiment, the entire student community took a leading role to bring forward this public agitation against the CTC as well as the Government.[25]

On June 27, a joint statement made by the leaders of the opposition parties, including the Communist Party of India (CPI), Praja Socialist Party (PSP), Revolutionary Socialist Party (RSP), Socialist Unity Centre of India (SUCI), Forward Bloc (FB), etc, opposed the government move to increase the fare. The same evening witnessed the formation of the Tram and Bus Fare Enhancement Resistance Committee comprising leaders of these political parties. Veteran Forward Bloc leader Hemanta Basu was its president, while Jyoti Basu (CPI), Subodh Banerjee (SUCI), Suresh Banerjee (PSP) and Satya Priya Banerjee (Marxist Forward Bloc) were the members. Eventually this committee came to be known popularly as Resistance Committee or Pratirodh Committee.[26]

The demonstration against fare rise started in full force

from the very first day of the fare hike, i.e. July 1, 1953. Hundreds of Resistance Committee volunteers, mainly young men, in their respective areas, called upon the people to refuse to pay the increased fare. They themselves boarded the trams and offered old fares.[27]

On the evening of July 2, Dr .B. C. Roy, the then Chief Minister of West Bengal, defended the increase of fare in indisputable terms. In a press message, he claimed that the fare structure for second class travellers, after the proposed increase, was perhaps the lowest in the world. In defence of the increase, the press note stated that the expenses of running the tram cars had "mounted tremendously" in the recent past and the government was compelled to support the proposed fare rise according to the provisions of the Calcutta Tramways Act of 1951. In his statement, the Chief Minister gave a clear hint of government "offensive to-combat violence", when he categorically commented that any case of default to pay the fare was punishable under law, and the government could not "sit idle in the face of such lawlessness on the part of the picketers".[28]

On 4th July, 1953, the general strike was observed through the West Bengal in protest of this issue. But, gradually the speed of this movement became sloth when the students started continuous strike in schools and colleges, thousands of students showed their rally and detention programme just before the Head Office of CTC located at Mission Row, Calcutta. Again, one student rally consisting of a large number of students followed the path of Writers' Building, the then Head Quarter of West Bengal and reaching at Writers' Building, they started shouting by delivering slogans—"Either revised the enhanced Tram fare or, leave the power". During that student rally before the writers' Building, police started action by tremendous lathi charge and discharging tear shells. As a result, a large number of students were seriously injured and the police arrested numerous numbers of students from that spot. Even the girl-students could not get relief from the police action which proved that the police authority never took care to save the prestige and honour of the holy educational institutions in totality. For an example, the police tortured on Sri Parimal Mukherjee, the then prominent leader of Students' Association affiliated to Praja Socialist Party within the premises of Ashutosh College. Even the Principal of the College could not get relief from the hands of the police. In spite of such police action and tortures, the student community created a remarkable history keeping themselves attached with this public movement against the Tram fare hike decision sponsored by the then Government.[29]

This added fuel to the fire and students throughout the city erected barricades over tram tracks, improvised with dustbins and bullock-carts. As the police set itself to the task of removing the barricades, it faced stiff resistance from the demonstrators, resulting in severe disturbances in Hazra, Kalighat, Chitpore and Bowbazar.[30]

Under new circumstances, the ruling party also could no longer remain inactive. On July 21, the West Bengal Provincial Congress Committee met at Congress Bhavan and decided to make all-out effort to "resist goondaism being committed in the name of Fare Increase Resistance Committee".[31] The mass meeting or the successive procession organised by the Congress failed to make any impact.

In different areas, barricades were set up by local youths to block the mobility of the forces of law and order, "spontaneously turning the paras into fortresses". Another new technique was adopted by the local youths, in face of severe repression by the military and police forces. They would demolish the bulbs of the street lamps or cut the electric wires and thereby plunge the whole area into darkness, making it difficult for the police and army to move about.[32] The Police and army atrocities throughout Calcutta were condemned everywhere. Manik Bandyopadhyay, the famous Bengali writer, disturbed at the police and army actions in the city on July 15 and 16, wrote his famous Chhara which was published in Swadhinata on July 17, 1953.[33]

The whole press, excepting the British-owned Statesman and the Congress organ Janasevak, harshly criticised the government activities. The Jugantar and the Ananda Bazar Patrika editorially supported the peoples' reaction against fare rise. But the Statesman in its editorial took a different stand. It was professedly sympathetic to those who were "genuinely upset by the increase in second class fare" and, at the same time, was convinced that the "people have a right to expect a fall and not a rise in the cost of living.[34]

Confused at the increasing intensity of the agitation and tramway men's decision of launching an indefinite strike on the one hand and reeling before the attack of the press on the other, the government sought the advice of the Press Advisory Council for a way out to neutralize the crisis. The Press Advisory Council, consisting of the editors of important newspapers, made three recommendations: (I) referring the question of fare to a tribunal, (2) withdrawal of Section 144 of Indian Penal Code from the city, and (3) release of all prisoners arrested in connection with fare increase resistance movement. Similar advice was given by a committee of prominent citizens, headed by Radha Binode Pal, the noted jurist.[35]

As the situation in Calcutta grew worse Dr. Bidhan Chandra Roy, the then Chief Minister of West Bengal, had to cut short his European tour and return home rather hurriedly. On July 31, Dr. B. C. Roy assured the leaders of the Resistance Committee that all their demands would be accepted. The Committee then decided to withdraw its demonstration. The Joint Strike Committee of the tram workers also called off the strike "in deference to the wishes of the travelling public" of Calcutta on the same day.[36]

This Tram fare movement widened the way of joint action of the united student movement.[37] In fact, if we go to the social picture of Calcutta in 1953, it may be found that due to innumerable number of homeless or refugee people, the streets, the slams were filled in by refugees. At the same time many new colonies were forcibly established, where the large number of refugees including their sons and daughters took shelter. These refugee students had strongly protested and participated against the tram fare hike. They were not in a position to bear 1 paise fare hike. If anyone meticulously would study the profile of the students, he or she would find that a lion segment of the students had come from the newly established colonies, slams etc. It means the refugee student participation was very much significant. In order to justify our contention, we can give example for students' agitation of the 1960 onwards. It appears from the profile of leadership of the agitation that most of the student leader either East Bengalis or refugees.

Another peculiar characteristics of the student participation of the tram fare hike was that the students of mofussil area either reluctant or non-interested. The contemporary Newspapers and Periodicals do not provide us any information of the mofussil students on tram fare hike movement. In 1953 West Bengal mofussil students was not prepared to expedite their solidarity on the issue of the Calcutta students.

Finally, the foreign owner of CTC was compelled to withdraw the decision of fare hike, side by side, the police authority also was bound to release all the students, labourers and workers who were arrested during this movement. Moreover, section 144 which was promulgated upon the city of Calcutta was also withdrawn to normalize the daily public life allowing all meetings, union activities etc. like earlier.[38]

Thus, the Calcutta trams played a leading role in generating a mass movement in Calcutta. In fact, small economic issue of fare rise was made the basis of a large-scale challenge to the forces of law and order. The fight against fare rise was basically a struggle against British capital. But the entire wave of mass resentment finally went also against the Congress regime of West Bengal.[39]

PARTICIPATION IN THE TEACHERS' MOVEMENT

In West Bengal the School Teachers organized a lot of movements, strikes and demonstrations soliciting early action on the part of the Government concerning enhancement of pay-scales, better service conditions, healthier allowances etc. The school teachers in those days were given very low pay- scale and they did not have service security. Their lives were a tale of melancholy. The eminent Bengali novelists like Bibhutibhusan Bandyopadhyay, Manoj Basu described poor quality of life, humiliations, and insecurity with consummate skill. The teachers obviously expected that in independent India their service conditions would be improved and they would enjoy a reasonable wage to survive. During the 1950s, All Bengal Teachers Association (ABTA) was the foremost organization of Secondary Teachers in West Bengal. But the Government did not respond to their demands. As a result, the teachers decided to go on movements. On 10th February, 1954 the Secondary Teachers of West Bengal under the guidance of ABTA started an indefinite cease of work and they planned a squatting before Raj Bhawan, Calcutta.[40] The leaders who have planned this movement were Monoranjan Sengupta, Satyapriya Roy, Hiren Roy, Sunil Mukherjee, Ajit Das, Bamandas Mandal, Anila Devi Bina Chaudhury etc. The direct action on the part of the teachers produced a strong public opinion in their favour. People from various walks of life went to the Esplanade area and acknowledged their support for the striking teachers.

As a mark of support for the demands of the secondary teachers the students had decided to propagate it vigorously among the general people. In every District of Bengal the leaders of BPSF, CB, and PSU etc. started propaganda in favour of the teachers. There was no one among the District in this state, where the student leaders did not promote the interests of the teachers. The students were assembled in different districts to aware the public about poorer condition of teachers. At this time a joint meeting of the teachers-students was held at the playground of Bolpur in support of the teachers' movement. In this meeting the presence of the general students of Santiniketan, Viswa Bharati was spectacular. Mr. Hiren Dasgupta, General Secretary, BPSF was the main speaker in this joint gathering. In the like manner so many meetings, demonstrations took place in the different parts of Calcutta as well as Districts by the students.[41]

As predictable, the Government tried to restrain this movement by applying force and in this process created an adverse reaction. There were cores of hot demonstrations, loot and arson, when the police arrested the ABTA and student leaders. Police opened firings and lathi charged which worsened the condition.[42] The arrested leaders were Hiren Dasgupta, General Secretary, BPSF; Rathin Mitra, Editor, The Student Magazine, Shyamal Roy; Shibdas Ghosh, General Sectary, SUCI; Sachin Sen, Councilor, Ballygunj, Kolkata; Mohit Moitra, Reporter; Dr. Suresh Banerjee, leader of PSP; Bhupal Basu, leader of FB; Sudhangshu Chaudhury and Nitai Basu, Student leaders. Last but not the least; Jyoti Basu was arrested just after leaving the Assembly.

On 17th February, 1954 the students called strike when they gheraoed the Bengal Legislative Assembly, the police resorted inhuman lathi charge and opened firing to disperse the rebellious students. In this police action one student was killed. To protest against this incident peoples from all walks of life came out on the streets in Calcutta. The Government had decided to tackle the movement by exerting force and even marched the Para-military force in the streets of Calcutta. With this worst situation, the government was bound to accept few demands of the teachers and declared that the rest may be discussed later on. After getting assurance from the Government, the leaders of ABTA withdrew their movement. Finally, Dr. Bidhan Chandra Roy, the then Chief Minister of West Bengal came to this entire episode, and he accepted most of the demands made by ABTA. After that ABTA's status reached a new height. ABTA leaders were also elected in the West Bengal Legislative Assembly.[43]

The West Bengal College and University Association (WBCUTA) also launched movements for numerous times. The Association demanded that in Government sponsored colleges, the practice of police verification of newly recruited teachers should be discontinued. Better pay-scale for teachers, introduction of a consistent pay scale, old age benefits, increased budgetary allocation for education; these points were demanded by WBCUTA. People from various corner of life supported their demands. The students also supported their demands and started to propagate it among the mass.[44] For example, in response to the call of WBCUTA, most of the teachers of the then Raiganj University College observed cease of work and the students supported them. It deserves to be mentioned that in Dinajpur this had been the first movement by the college teachers.[45]

As a result of these movements, the teachers and non-teaching employees of West Bengal now are enjoying attractive pay scale, retirement benefits and pension after their retirement. Regional language has become the medium of instruction in a majority of schools and colleges. The University and College teachers now enjoy a larger amount of autonomy, as because the University Acts have been revised. The numbers of schools, colleges and Universities have increased. But the absences of suitable monitoring, lack of inspection, decline in social accountability and awareness have unfavorably and adversely affected our schools and colleges. The teachers should dedicate more time and attention to their students.

PARTICIPATION IN THE ANTI-MERGER MOVEMENT OF BENGAL AND BIHAR

In 1956, Dr. Bidhan Chandra Roy, the then Chief Minister of West Bengal and Srikrishna Singh, the then Chief Minister of Bihar began endeavoring to unite both the states into one single whole. To protest against this attempt the whole of Bengal rose up in unison.[46] When demands for restructuring of states on the basis of language twisted it into an all India movement, the Union Government was strained to appoint a State Re-Organization Commission consisting of Sarder K. M. Panikkar, Justice Fazal Ali and Pandit H. N. Kunjru. Before independence the Congress committed itself to the model of linguistic states and full provincial autonomy. Bengali speaking people of the adjacent states like Bihar, Assam and Orissa were excited to return to west Bengal. In Manbhum, the Lok Sevak Sangha which had a strong mass base was very enthusiastic on the point that Bengali speaking areas of Bihar would be merged with West Bengal. Consequently, when the two Chief Ministers projected the creation of a new state of ‘Purba Desh’, the opponent parties including students strongly reacted against this budge and organized meetings and demonstrations decrying the merger proposal.[47] Many youth and students participated in this movement. From this time onwards the allied students-youths movement began acquiring a distinct and permanent form in Bengal.[48]

The agitators tinted a rather gloomy future of the projected bilingual state of Purba Desh in which Bengali culture, Bengali language, in short the heritage of Bengal, would be packed down. As projected, the Government did not take recourse to oppressive measures this time, rather the Government tried to generate a favourable public opinion by a skilful exercise of the mass media of information.[49] In April 1956, two by-elections were held on the issue of Bengal-Bihar merger, in which two seats were won by the anti-Government candidates. To consider the gravity of the situation Dr. B. C. Roy bowed down to this strong public opinion and unilaterally withdrew his proposal.[50]

SUMMING UP

These popular protest movements and the participation of the students in it had created a relatively autonomous space in the minds of the people. Sometimes the movements were peaceful and sometimes violent. Actually the popular protest movements broke out after the end of World War II, which marked the beginning of a wave of popular protests in Bengal organized mainly by the left forces. These movements took almost spontaneous shape in those days. The effect of the movements was so intense that it changed the political complexion of the state.

NOTES AND REFERENCES

1. Chakraborty, D. (2006): Leftist Student Movement in Bengal: 1935-1947, Published Ph.D. Thesis (in Bengali) namely 'Banglay Bampanthi Chhatra Andolan', Published by Boiwala, Kolkata, pp. 134-137.
2. Sarkar S. (1983): Modern India: 1885-1947, Macmillan, New Delhi, pp. 453-454.
3. Chakraborty, D. (2006), op. cit., p. 135.
4. Ray, Ramashray (1971): Patterns of Political Instability, Economic and Political Weekly, Annual Number, January, 1971, p. 295.
5. Ray, S. (2007): Marxist Parties of West Bengal: 1947-2001, Progressive, Kolkata, p. 33.

6. Dasgupta, H. and Adhikary H. (1993 & 2008): Rajnaitik Poto Bhumite Bharatiya Upamahadesher Chhatra Andolan(In Bengali), School for People, Medinipore, and Radical Impression, Kolkata, pp. 162-163.

7. Dasgupta, H. and Adhikary H. (1993 & 2008), op. cit., p. 163.

8. Dasgupta, H. and Adhikary, H. (1993 & 2008): Rajnaitik Poto Bhumite Bharatiya Upamahadesher Chhatra Andolan(In Bengali), School for People, Medinipore, and Radical Impression, Kolkata, p. 100.

9. The UGC Report on the Problem of Student Indiscipline in Indian Universities, 1960, p. 10 & Sarkar S. N. : Student Unrest: A Socio-Psychological Study, Indian Book Exchange, Kolkata, 1974, p.140.

10. The UGC Report on the Problem of Student Indiscipline in Indian Universities, 1960, p. 10 & Sarkar ,S. N. : Student Unrest: A Socio-Psychological Study, Indian Book Exchange, Kolkata, 1974, p.140.

11. www.gandhiforchildren.org

12. Dasgupta, H. and Adhikary H. (1993 & 2008), op. cit., p. 164.

13. Sarvepalli, G. (1979): Jawaharlal Nehru, Jonathan Cape, London, pp. 16-17, and also see www.googleweblight.com/ www.wikipedia.org

14. Ibid.

15. Dasgupta, H. and Adhikary H. (1993 & 2008), op. cit., p. 167.

16. Chakraborti, P. K. (1999): The Marginal Men, Naya Udyog, Kolkata, p. 1.

17. The Amrita Bazar Patrika, Dated. 05.06.1948.

18. Dasgupta, H. and Adhikary H. (1993 & 2008), p. 168.

19. See Nehru's Statement in Parliament- "Recently there were unfortunate clashes between some students and others and the police in Calcutta, and during these clashes, hand grenades and bomb were used against the police, and the public property, such as buses and tram cars, were destroyed." Select Documents: Oxford University Press, 1959, p. 536.

20. Ray, S. (2007), op. cit., p. 124.
21. Dasgupta, H. and Adhikary H. (1993 & 2008), op. cit., p. 169.
22. Dasgupta, H. and Adhikary H. (1993 & 2008), op. cit., pp. 169-170.
23. Guha Roy, S. (1990): Fare Hike and Urban Protest; Calcutta Crowd in 1953, Economic and Political Weekly, December 29, 1990.
24. Guha Roy, S. (1990), Ibid.
25. Dasgupta, H. and Adhikary H. (1993 & 2008), op. cit., pp. 172-177.
26. Ananda Bazar Patrika, Dated. 28.06.1953.
27. Guha Roy, S. (1990), Ibid.
28. The Statesman, Dated. 03.07.1953.
29. Acharya, A. (ed, 1998 & 2014): Sat-Sattarer Chhatra Andolan(in Bengali), Anustup, Kolkata, & Enlarged Edition, pp. 29-30.
30. The Statesman, Dated. 16.07.1953.
31. The Statesman, Dated. 13.07.1953.
32. New Age, November, 1953, p.76.
33. Swadhinata, July 17, 1953.
34. The Statesman, Dated. 04.07.1953.
35. New Age, November, 1953, p.77.
36. Ibid.
37. Ibid.
38. Dasgupta, H. and Adhikary H. (1993 & 2008), op. cit., pp. 172-177.
39. Guha Roy, S. (1990).
40. Ray, S. (2007), p. 130.
41. Dasgupta, H. and Adhikary H. (1993 & 2008), op. cit., pp. 181-182.
42. Siksha O Sahitya, Journal of ABTA, April Issue, 1958.
43. Ray, S. (2007), pp. 130-131.

44. Ray, S. (2007), op. cit., p. 131.
45. Frontier, The Weekly, Vol. 47, No. 9, September 7-13, 2014, An Article namely "Communist Impact: Leftism in Undivided Dinajpur" written by Swapan Kumar Pain, pp. 14-15.
46. Ibid. p. 14.
47. Ray, S. (2007), op. cit., p. 129.
48. Frontier: op. cit., p. 14.
49. Dr. Bidhan Chandra Roy's Statement on 3rd May 1956: "So far as I am concerned, I feel that I should withdraw this proposal and bow down to the bar of public opinion." Saroj Chakraborty: with Dr. B. C. Roy and other Chief Ministers, Published by Bensons, Calcutta, 1974, p. 317.
50. The Statesman (Calcutta Daily), April 10-20, 1956, see also Assembly Proceedings, pp. 50-58, 61.2.54.

4

Impact of Global Student Movement: A Debate

The emergence of the global student movement has been one of the most dramatic and noble social phenomenon of the 1960s throughout the world. To understand totally about the evolution of this movement, we have to have some ideas about the international socio-political perspective and the continuous student uprising of the then world at large.

There is a continuous debate among the scholars regarding the vibrant students' movement of Post-Partition Era especially the 60s. Whatever those students' movements were fully in right way or, in wrong, rather it was more important to judge these movements in the light of national and international causation or incidents. It was established that in one hand, the main cause of the student movements during the 6os and 70s was the socio-economic crisis of the country, on the other hand, there were so many living examples to draw inspiration from the movements of the students of France and Germany against capitalism, uncompromised students' movements of Europe and America, the Vietnamese Liberation movement against American imperialism, the cultural movements of Communist China etc. Observing the scarcity of food, dress, poverty and discrimination of common people in their lives, behind the extravagant life style of the elitist of America and Europe created adverse reaction in the mind of the students from which faith of the entire student community upon existing system was shattered down into pieces. In addition to that the student community also came to know about the facts of suffered and poverty-stricken people of the Third World which intensified the momentum of this movement. This disparity in the socio-economic fabric of the society of the two different continents leads to a depression among the students who spoilt themselves by consuming ganja-opium in the Third World Countries, on the other hand, the conscious students group raised vehement protest against the existing ruling set up, which was also reflected among the students of West Bengal as well as throughout India.[1] The contemporary global students' movement and the various issues left a vibrant impact upon the student community of West Bengal at large.

MOVEMENTS OF THE 1960S: ISSUES

Mr. Asim Chattopadhyay, Pro-revolutionary student leader of West Bengal during the 1960s and 1970s, traced out following two factors[2] for which the student movement began in West Bengal.

1. **Socio-economic factor:** The main reasons for the student agitation in the Western World were due to social, economic and political issues. There was sort of pressure upon the young students in the age of the monopoly of capital accumulation. In that age of the enhancement of productive power, the modern industrial and technological acumen played its part. Modern society as a matter of fact began producing various commodities in massive quantities and in return it began demanding from us such a man who would be always ignorant, unconscious and passive outside his field of activity. When this demand is fulfilled the man wanted by the society becomes isolated from others and such man began to be born in the teeth of tremendous opposition from the opponents of it. And in course of time the opponents begin to unite, although in a desperate alliance to give vent to their grievances in

the aggressive manner. In point of fact this is the inevitable problem of opulence and indiscriminate prosperity.

2. **Political factor:** With the end of the World War II and the Cold War, there was the process of elimination of the Sino-Russian bi-polar politics. At that time a remarkable evolution was marked in political values of the student community for making an end to democratic system which was continued in the name of preservation of orthodox social structure. As the Vietnam War during that time was not sufficient to create an environment in favour of the communist struggle to lead a sizeable student movement forward, it was quite natural to turn the attention of the student-youth community to the socio-economic crisis of the country during that period, which leads to create a tumultuous wave for students' agitation.

In spite of this, the author admitted that none of these influences like social, economic and political was reflected for the student movement of our country.

From the very beginning of the 1960s the organized students' movement can be marked in different countries. Gradually the wave of this movement spread in several places and in 1968 it was reached its highest height. In the same time, the students' movement got momentum in the different parts of the Globe, for which the movement takes an international shape.[3] We observed that in different countries the students' movements were on different issues and demands, the News Media of the then world gave special attention for focusing the student movement and its issues of Europe and America. The different incidents which were taking place in one country started to cast its influence on the movements of other countries. Although, these movements had no focal point, the movement of 1968 attended the international shape from the historical point of view. The students' movement of the capitals, cities and towns of different countries of the Free World was named as 'Student Revolt' or in somewhere as 'Student Revolution' by the writers, scholars and historians of Western World. In many cases, we can mark some different opinions for using these two terms. In this regard, many scholars also mentioned the statement of Mao-Tse-Tung delineating the student movement as a part of peoples' movement. Mao-Tse-Tung once said "The student movement is a part of the whole peoples' movement. The upsurge of the student movement will inevitably promote an upsurge of the whole peoples' movement."[4]

Whatever may be the impact of using two separate terms like Revolt and Revolution, actually the students' agitation in the Free World transformed into a Student Revolt, rather than a Student Revolution.

In all countries of the world, students' movement was not originated in the same manner. There were so many issues and differences of these movements. In spite of several issues, there were some radical features and similarity in these movements which could be marked for getting importance in all types of student movement everywhere. Among these factors the main and common point was specifically, the growing consciousness against imperialism and its influences. Apart from all these, the student community organized movements to solve different educational problems in the existing socio-economic frame work of their own countries. The students also participated in the various peasant and labour movements.[5] Moreover, the vibrant student movements across the world was fortified mainly on the basis of deep rooted tumultuous political movements and its crisis which energized and was the basic issues for getting a wide impact during the contemporary period.

The movement of the students' started in the 1960s for several interconnected reasons. One of them was the convergence between affluence and other demographic, technological, institutional, and ideological factors.[6] This process took place between 1945 and 1975. Another was the demographic factors and the characteristics of the 1940s i.e. the famous "baby boom," the extremely high birth rate during that period. This spectacular increase resulted in high percentages of young people in 1960s. The 1960s were different from the 1940s and 1950s, in the logic that a number of transformations taking place to arise that shaped an altered reality. The living standards of the people started increasing gently and a new trend called "consumerism" started. On the other hand, the most characteristic feature that marked and defined the decade was the series of powerful and violent political protests and confrontations. Generally, the protagonists of these events were mainly the students and youths.

The year 1968 was the most important of the 1960s because it had a significant impact on the student community. According to Marwick, the young people, specifically the students, who did not reveal any interest in politics and who were resistant to radical principles based on Marxist theory up to that point[7], the student agitation in the West could be described as collective actions against absolutism and totalitarianism. At this time the students created stern disruptions in societies and shook political systems worldwide such as France, West Germany, Italy, England, Czechoslovakia, the USA and many other countries. The importance of these movements in terms of global expansion is one of their most deep-seated and major characteristics.[8] The Third World countries also faced movements created by students and youths. These movements were more powerful in the developed countries of Western Europe, the United States, and Japan, but many Third World and Eastern European countries had intense movements as well.

WESTERN STUDENT MOVEMENT: USA

In the Western Countries, a radical way of student movement brought out in different universities. It began in the early 1960s. The first demonstration of the student participation in various social issues took place in the USA. The student of the USA actively participated in civil rights movement. This movement made the Berkeley Revolt at the University of California in 1964. The radical students of USA did not confine themselves to the right of free speech in the campus or academic issues, but also involved other socio-economic and political issues. In 1965, the students formed 'Independent Committee on Vietnam' (ICV) in Columbia University to protest against American involvement in Vietnam War. The main cause for escalation of American participation to the Vietnam War was the source of inspiration of student movement in many universities. The student also protested to Columbia's lack of help to its surrounding neighborhood.[9] The Black students of America have supported the demand for Black power. They demanded the recruitment of more Negro students and teachers and a curriculum that predominantly featured Afro-American history.[10] The involvement of students in the USA played a vital role in the American life and society.

Before the decades of sixties Latin American students were extremely active for their education and politics. The main cause of their active participation lies in the history of university reform and broadly the political and social structure of their countries. They got the inspiration from Cordoba Manifesto of 1918. The students of Latin America thought that the academic reform is itself an inadequate objective and can only be seen suitably achieved by the transformation of the whole society in which the university functions. If the society has not been changed, the liberty and rights of all students are insecure. So, that the Latin American countries especially Bolivia, Cuba,

Panama, Peru and Venezuela students have declared war against American imperialism.[11]

STUDENT MOVEMENT OF ENGLAND

The student movement of England had its own characteristics. Their movement was related to left ideology. They were very much influenced by the writings of Herbert Marcuse, Mao Tse Tung and Che Guevara. The British student movement came into limelight in the political events of Suez Canal Crisis of 1956 and the Campaign for Nuclear Disarmament of 1958. The students fought for educational reforms demanding satisfactory student participation in the decision making process and curriculum development.[12] The centers of these movements were Guildford, Croydon, and Hornsey. In 1968, a vigorous student movement broke out in London School of Economics (LSE). The radical students of LSE propagated that "British students this year have watched their counterparts aboard make history....What are the prospects for militant students in Britain? So far the beginning of student struggle have been encouraging but scattered....The LSE socialist society has recently taken an important initiative by calling for revolutionary student movement. Such an organization answers an urgent need."[13] There were so many reasons for protesting inspired by many songs by the Beatles led by John Lennon, Paul McCartney, Ringo Starr and George Harrison.

STUDENT MOVEMENT OF FRANCE

The student movement in France was violent and massive, but they also had a distinct character. The main centers of the French student movement were Sorbonne University, Toulouse University, Nanterre University, Strasbourg University etc. The May Movement of 1968 in France led initially by students and teachers. It was a turning point in French politics. A lion segment of the students of Nanterre moved against inadequate grants for University. They also demanded cultural and other facilities. Soon the movement spread over provincial Universities like Aixen Province, Bordeaux, Caen, Dijon, Grenoble, Montpellier, Rouen etc.[14] The students did not confine their movement into the educational institutions, they involved in the movements to shops, factories and work places. The students and workers joined together in the different movements. This student movement of France rocked the whole fabric of capitalistic society.[15]

STUDENT MOVEMENT OF GERMANY

In the Post-Sixties, the German student movement took place against insufficient public funds for higher education, exploitation of the capitalist countries, US involvement in Vietnam issue and democratization of the University. The focal point of the German student movement was the Free University of West Berlin. In 1965, the leftist student of this University invited Mr. Erich Kuby, a noted journalist believed in leftist ideology, to deliver a lecture in a student programme. But the University Authority refused to allow Mr. Kuby in the University Campus. The students were forced to conduct the programme outside the University. This incident foreboded the student upheaval in West Berlin.[16] The Berlin student also agitated against the Shah of Iran whose regime was marked by repression.

STUDENT MOVEMENT OF SPAIN

The student movement of Spain in the sixties had been connected both to the crisis of Franco's Regime and different issues of the university education. After the establishment of fascist rule in Spain during 1930s the education system of Spain was neglected and the government was very much antagonistic to the intellectual class. Naturally, the intellectual class and the students in particular demanded the modernization of the university education through much needed reforms. After 1964 the Spanish fascist government started to suppress the student agitation by using state machinery. The student movement for free unions escalated into broader political issues. The student did not confine their movement within educational institutions; they also showed their solidarity to the weaker sections of the society. In 1967, students in Madrid demanded workers' representation on a committee deliberating a change in trade union laws. A section of students thought that the condition of the workers was not an isolated phenomenon; it was a social problem and symbol of oppressive government. Finally, the student and worker solidarity was consummated in the year of 1968 by declaring 3 days national struggle.[17] So, it may be said that the Spanish student movement had initiated an open popular movement against a fascist government and they established the demands of the worker section of the society before the Franco Government.

STUDENT MOVEMENT OF RUSSIA

Soviet Russia had witnessed a long student movement since 19th century. The Russian Revolutionary Movement of 19th century consisted to a considerable degree of University students. But in the Post-War period there was no available student movement other than De-Stalinization campaign. One significant movement that played by the students along with the intellectuals in the post-war period was the reforms of the Soviet Society.[18]

STUDENT MOVEMENTS OF ASIA, AFRICA AND LATIN AMERICA

The students played a significant role in the States of Asia, Africa and Latin America. In many Asian and African Countries they were the forefront of the nationalist movements and many of the student leaders achieved political leadership in the Post-

Independence Government. In Japan, the student played a historic role in any world point of view. The character of the Japanese student movement was anti-Americanism.[19] The most important political upsurge of student occurred in 1960 in Japan against the renewal of the security treaty between Japan and America. In 1968, other aggressive conflicts erupted over foreign and domestic issues. A number of student demonstrations against the Vietnamese War clashed constantly with police and to continue their momentum because of unprecedentedly solid technical preparation. The students rallied to the demonstrations well-armed with helmets, shields and javelins. The forging of worker-peasant-student alliance against the government and against the American aggression in Vietnam was an important step ahead in student political action. If we compare the Bengal students' movement with the Japanese students movement, it may be said that Japanese students were more politically organized and were less utopian. In West Bengal the students were more utilized by the leaders of the existing political parties and most of the political parties had direct link with their student wing as a result of which student movement lost its independent character.[20]

In Post Second World War China had to face a series of student movement. After Chinese Revolution of 1949, the Communist Party of China promoted the students in the mass movements controlled by the party and Youth League. Millions of students were involved in Red Guard Movement, Long Marches and many other struggles throughout China. In the recent past the student activism in China had been got crucial political importance. It had been quite different in character from the past. Mao-Tse-Tung was always hopeful for the ability of students and youths. He compared the students and youths with the 'Morning Sun'.[21] According to Mao the world belongs to the youth and students must be trusted and kept in confidence. The Chinese students and youths have always played a very important role in the different critical phases of the Chinese political history. Students also fought for economic and social modernization. According to Joseph Fisher, "the poor prospects of employment following the degree are fundamental to the insecurity of the University youth. Since the intellectual and humane values of education do not interest most of the students and the pursuit of learning is rare, the dim practical prospects further the demoralization and alienation of the students."[22] In most of the African countries the student movement began during colonial rule. They fought for national independence. This tradition has sustained in the post-independence period also.

Flacks distinguished two main features of these movements in order to justify their international character. These are the simultaneity of the outbursts and the general attributes they have in terms of method and strategy. He argued that these movements were international in range and he steadily believed that they were a phenomenon that did not originate in the 1960s, but existed beforehand during the 19th century in various countries, such as Russia, China, and in Latin-America. Moreover, it was rational for such movements to show, in order to oppose tsars, war-lords, and dictators. He used a phrase to sum it up: "the feeling that there is something new about generational revolt is not accurate in global terms". [23] Siegfried too puts it "...it is questionable whether the description of the network of the events of 1968 as a global revolution is accurate." He justifies this point of view by noting that the series of events did not have instant and profound results in the form of changes to any economic or political systems, and that in a number of cases they did not even have an impact on existing governments.

To the progressive of those days around the world Vietnam and its liberation war against the Yankee imperialism was a living symbol of indomitable revolutionary velour. At that time

Soviet Union deviated from the revolutionary ideal. That is why it was never considered to be a vibrant source of inspiration to the revolutionaries. A sort of aberration took place in the revolutionary ideology of Soviet Union. As a result of that China came to the force to fill up this position without any delay. All the roads of Peking and Sanghai were full of millions singing, dancing and acting in unison; red guards sent waves of their inspiring clarion call to the other side of China, beyond its frontiers.[24]

NEW CHARACTERISTICS OF THE MOVEMENT

A new characteristic began to feature in the revolutionary beside the students of Berlin, Rome, Stugart, Milan, London and Paris organized scores of students' demonstrations. In America Students tore 'Draft Cards' of the soldiers to whom the joining of army was made compulsory by this. The Blacks were agitating for their rights and after the assassination of Martin Luther they got an extra fillip from all these movements that began to shake the whole of America. Above all, the students of Paris created a perfectly revolutionary situation in which labourers, peasants and clerks took part. Due to this agitation the destiny of France became uncertain for a few days. The situation reached to such height that the call of one single left party was enough to cause a country-wide flare-up.[25] Inspiration from all these movements of different cities and towns of the world lent to the student movement of Bengal such a novel dimension.

Any active students' movement will concern itself with collective action on its own ground: students can occupy their colleges, they cannot occupy factories. Student power is not primarily a matter of constitutional rights, but rather of the students' autonomous capacity for mobilization and struggle. By engaging in struggles with University or College authorities, students can make inroads on established power, but these gains will only be lasting where the consciousness of the student enemas has been aroused. In fact, student power has only acquired a truly revolutionary character where students have rejected the notion that higher education is a world of its own.[26]

The student movements in France, West Germany, Japan and elsewhere have all soon discovered the necessity of breaking the isolation which bourgeois society imposes on students in the form of privilege. These movements have reached out to all the potentially revolutionary forces in the society in part and in the world as a whole. The former type of solidarity has often provided the initial stimulus for student actions while the latter has usually become an overriding preoccupation after the student revolutionaries have already achieved some success.[27]

IMPACT

All these student movements in the different parts of the Globe have spread its tentacles in India especially in West Bengal. The students of Bengal went in favour of left and communist leadership in response to the call of battle against the fetish of imperialism. Right from 1945 Calcutta had been witnessing student movements in support of Vietnam Liberation Movement. It was in Calcutta, the liberals of 19th century Bengal celebrated the victory of the Paris Revolution. The Bolshevik Revolution thrilled the young men and women in Bengal. In 1935 in this city of West Bengal the Anti Fascist League became active.[28] So there is no doubt in it that the mammoth assembles of thousands of students in the last part of the 1960s such as Student Rebellion in Germany, 1967; Suez War Oil Crisis of 1967, Students' Convention against the aggression of Vietnamese Tate, 1968; May Day, 1969 etc. took place on a few international issues.

Side by side with West Bengal, India too as a whole was not an exception. Here revolutionary ideas were getting momentum very rapidly. Strike of labourers, peasants protest disintegration of the ruling party in 1967 forebodes that India was very quickly approaching to the ultimate catastrophe. But when the opportune moment arrived, students, youths and peasant became successful in achieving their end but other sections of the society displayed inability in marching ahead and striking hard against the oppressors. Then it was seen that the students and youths decided to go forward with their shoulder together under the impulse but no other sections of people sided with them. When they did not get any support from different sections of the society they decided to go ahead single handed and the consequence was the death knell of the movement. This appeared to be the universal destiny of the student movement of the time.[29]

In fact, the story of the 1960s is a long tale of frustration of a romantic dream. For a long period of time the pre-independent India began weaving a vast network of an independent India with its expectation of emancipation of this country from the British Rule. During the dark age of British Rule a myth about independence gradually began to develop in the mind of young people of India. This myth was like a wonderful lamp appeared to be miraculously luminous which would bring bright light of prosperity to the traditionally poverty stricken and starving India. The hard earned independence brought about an ample of hope and expectations. But they were very soon disillusioned by the apathetic attitude of the ruling class. In this decade it became clear that we had a yoke of imperialist vestige chain of feudalistic oppression. Still we had to prosper with a view to making limited capitalistic development. Our movement for the capital formation suffered a serious setback in volatile economic process because of the indomitable pressure of imperialism and the shackles of feudalism. The fact began to loom large that in the region of a decadent capitalism our experimental march through the capitalistic way has ended in the birth of a perverted, perfunctory capitalism. The consequence of this experiment told upon the already decaying life of the peasant and labourers. This perspective of the 1960s became the breeding ground of a series of student and youth uprising. From this time student movement of a new type and with a new direction started.[30]

From the statement made by Kisan Chatterjee, it becomes clear that at that time students did not join socio-economic movements all of a sudden. They were stimulated by the movements of the 1960s of the USA, England, France, Germany, Italy, China, Russia and Afro-Asian countries. In India, especially in West Bengal, the student movements became too militant after 1962.[31]

SUMMING UP

The Global student movements of the sixties had created an adverse reaction on the youth minds, from which faith of the students upon existing system was shattered down into pieces. This adverse reaction reflected in a section of students of West Bengal of the sixties. But, it was a long tale of frustration of a romantic dream. The fact is that from this time onwards the student movements of Bengal had started a new direction.

NOTES AND REFERENCES

1. Acharya, A. (ed, 1998 & 2014): Shat-Sattarer Chhatra Andolan(In Bengali), An Article namely 'Shat Dashaker Chhatra Andolan' Written by Saibal Mitra, Anustup, Kolkata, enlarged edition, p. 77.
2. Acharya, A. (ed, 1998 & 2014): Shat-Sattarer Chhatra Andolan(in Bengali), An Article namely 'Shat Dashaker Yuva-Chhatra Andolan' written by Asim Chatterjee, Anustup, Kolkata, & Enlarged Edition, pp. 13-14.

3. Dasgupta, H. and Adhikary, H. (1993 & 2008): Rajnaitik Poto Bhumite Bharatiya Upamahadesher Chhatra Andolan(In Bengali), School for People, Medinipore and Radical Impression, Kolkata, pp., 295-296.
4. Barbara and John E. (1969): Long March, Short Spring: The Student Uprising at Home and Abroad, First Modern Paperbak Edition, USA, p. 159.
5. Dasgupta, H. and Adhikary, H. (1993 & 2008), pp. 296-298.
6. Marwick, A.: Youth Culture and the Cultural Revolution of the Long Sixties in Scheldt, and Siegfried, D. eds. Between Marx and Coca-Cola: Youth Cultures in Changing European Societies, 1960-1980. Bergman Books, pp.39-58 & Angelika Mitropoulos, Cardiff University, found at www.e-ir.inf
7. Marwick, A.: Ibid.
8. Siegfried, D.: Understanding 1968: Youth Rebellion, Generational Change and Postindustrial Society in Scheldt, and Siegfried, D. eds. Between Marx and Coca-Cola: Youth Cultures in Changing European Societies, 1960-1980. Bergman Books, p. 61 & Angelika Mitropoulos, Cardiff University, found at www.e-ir.inf
9. Altbach, P.G. (ed, 1968): Indian and the World University Crisis, Asia Publishing House, p. 18, found at www.shodhganga.inflibnet.ac.in
10. Lipset, S.M. (1969): Student Activities: A Profile, The American Review, Vol. XIII, No. 4, 1969, p. 18, found at www.shodhganga.inflibnet.ac.in
11. Ghosh, Shyamal Kumar (2014): Naxalite Student Youth Movement of 1970, Sopan Publisher, Kolkata, pp. 113-116.
12. www.shodhganga.inflibnet.ac.in
13. Barbara and John, E. (1969), p. 114.
14. Dasgupta, H. and Adhikary, H. (1993 & 2008), 318-319.
15. www.shodhganga.inflibnet.ac.in
16. Dasgupta, H. and Adhikary, H.(1993 & 2008), p. 304.
17. Ghosh, Shyamal Kumar (2014): op. cit. pp. 123-125.

18. David, B. (1960): Observation on University Students, Daedalus, Vol. LXXXLX, No. 3, p. 58 found at www.shodhganga.inflibnet.ac.in
19. Altbach, P.G. (ed), (1968), p.11.
20. Ghosh, Shyamal Kumar (2014): Naxalite Student Youth Movement of 1970, Sopan Publisher, Kolkata, pp. 141-142.
21. Quotations from Chairman Mao (1967): Foreign Language Press, Peking and also see Ghosh Shyamal Kumar (2014): Naxalite Student Youth Movement of 1970, Sopan Publisher, Kolkata, pp. 117-120.
22. Joseph, F. (1963): The University Students in South and South-East Asia, Minerva, Vol. II, No. 1, Autumn, p. 51.
23. Flacks, R.: Social and Cultural Meanings of Student Revolt: Some informal comparative observations, Social Problems 17(3), p.341 & Angeliki Mitropoulou, Cardiff University, found at www.e-ir.inf
24. Mills, C. W. (1959): The Sociological Imagination, Pelican, p. 161.
25. Cockburn, A. & Blackburn, R. (1969): Student Power: Problems, Diagnosis, Action, Penguin, England, p. 14.
26. Cockburn, A. & Blackburn, R. (1969) : Ibid.
27. Acharya, A. (ed, 1998 & 2014): Shat-Sattarer Chhatra Andolan(In Bengali), An Article namely 'Shat Dashaker Yuva-Chhatra Andolan' written by Asim Chatterjee, Anustup, Kolkata, enlarged edition, p. 13.
28. Acharya, A. (ed, 1998 & 2014): Shat-Sattarer Chhatra Andolan (in Bengali), An Article namely 'Banglar Bidrohi Yuva-Chhatra Andolan' written by Ranabir Samaddar, Anustup, Kolkata, enlarged edition, pp. 147-148.
29. Acharya, A. (ed, 1998 & 2014): Ibid .
30. An Interview with Kishan Chatterjee, Veteran Student Leader of 60s, NBU, Dated. 22.01.2007.
31. Ibid.

5

Role of Students during Economic Crisis: The Historic Food Movement of Bengal (1959-1966)

In the present chapter an attempt has been made to highlight the movement of the students in West Bengal during the tumultuous period of 1959-1966. After Partition of India West Bengal has to face a series of problems as a newly born state i.e. political instability, economic problem, problems of immigration and migration created an untoward situation throughout West Bengal.

After independence, till the 1960s, student movement did not occur anywhere in India comprehensively as was apprehended. But after the 60s the embryo of the students' disaffection matured into a decisive shape. The main reasons were the internal political and social ferment and very shocking economic crisis.[1]

SOCIO-ECONOMIC FABRIC OF INDIA AS REFLECTED IN THE REPORT OF RADHAKRISHNAN COMMISSION

In 1948, the Radhakrishnan Commission was constituted for the upliftment and betterment of University education. The commission submitted its Report in 1949 and in it the weakness of the socio-economic fabric of the then India became distinctly clear. The Report at the page 374 reads like this: "The boarding arrangements tie up closely with discipline. Poor and unwholesome food not only breeds malnutrition and disease but can become a centre of seething discontent. No single factor has a more vital effect upon the atmosphere and morale of a College or a University than the prevalent conditions under which students live. Convenient and comfortable quarters for study and sleep, sufficient and whole some food at low cost, are essential component to good spirit and the best progress in University work. Unfortunately most Universities and Colleges in India do not have adequate residential and dinning facilities for students. As a general rule, only a small fraction of the student finds accommodation in hostels".[2]

THE FOOD MOVEMENT OF 1959

Before the outset of the 1960s, the historic Food Movement in Calcutta along with the whole state of West Bengal shocked the people of Bengal. This Food Movements took a serious turn in 1959 and 1966. It was one of the most significant instances of mass movements in West Bengal. Dr. Sibaji Pratim Basu(2012) compared these movements with Charles Tilly's conceptions of 'contentious politics' and 'social movements' which originated in Europe in the eighteenth century and broadened all over the World in the following centuries through colonialism, trade and migration. He also found certain 'rhizomatic' tendencies – a term borrowed from Deluze and Guattari – in these movements as they evinced creation of their own structures and functions without much contribution from the 'vertical leadership.' Dr. Basu contextualized the Food Movement of 1959 in the backdrop of the famine in Bengal in 1943, the consequent peasant mobilizations in the late 1940s and the corrupt and inadequate public distribution system in post-independence West Bengal. The failure of the government to secure and distribute food grains together with the increasing population pressure after partition led to massive hoarding and black marketing which synthetically increased the food price. The opposition leaders of Bengal took a twine policy in this regard. They brought the issue of food paucity inside the State Assembly and thereby, drew public and media attention. Secondly, as a tactic of organizing anti-government mass movements, they formed various issue-based committees like the Price Increase and Famine Resistance Committee (PIFRC) for broader public support.[3] The PIFRC had played a historic role during the food movement.

At this critical juncture Union Food Minister, A. P. Jain visited Calcutta on 26.04.1959 to inquire the situation. He met the Chief Minister at his residence and later told the reporters that "food situation in West Bengal was easy, smooth and comfortable."[4]After this announcement, the public outcry throughout the state began to high. The common people wanted rice to be seized from the hoarded stocks of the big stockiest and dealers and sold through government or semi government agents at reasonable price. The English Daily, Amrita Bazar Patrika, which was growing crucial in course of the movement wrote in its editorial on 24.06.1959, "To withdraw an order under the statutory law on the plea of inability to enforce is nothing short of admitting the impotency of the administration....The Chief Minister now looks in retrospect and realizes the un-wisdom of the price control policy. But what is the prospect before us? He hopes that the withdrawal of control would improve the market availability of rice and paddy and also bring down their prices....This optimism is not supported by logic....The bulk of stocks are now in the hands of big dealers and producers who had hoarded them, despite anti-hoarding law, with a view to make larger profits. Naturally, they cannot be expected to disgorge their hoards competitively after decontrol to bring about a slump in prices....If, in the face of all these, the government contends that decontrol decision has been taken in public interest, the conclusion is inevitable that in the eye of the popular government, their interests are safer in the hands of profiteers and black marketers than in those of their chosen representatives." In the same column, the ABP also cautioned the government 'this retreat by the government will further embolden the anti social elements to fleece the public more openly and defiantly. And true to the anticipation of the opposition and editorials of some of the news dailies, the government's hope of release of hoarded rice and paddy upon the withdrawal of price control proved premature and unfounded'. [5]

On August 31, 1959, food marchers came to Calcutta from the adjoining Districts of Howrah, Hooghly, 24 Parganas, Nadia, Burdwan and Medinipur and gathered in the Esplanade area to protest against soaring prices of food grains and other essential commodities. The demonstrators were all along peaceful but the police suddenly encircled them and without giving any warning took recourse to severe lathi charges. Calcutta went wild over this incident, tram cars and buses were burnt and the police had to fire 447 rounds in Calcutta and Howrah. Strike calls were given by the left parties. According to their estimate, 80 persons were killed as a result of police firing.[6] Sudhir Roy Chowdhury, a PSP, MLA said on the floor of the West Bengal Legislative Assembly, "It is no wonder if there is any sporadic eruption of the volcano that the Government has spread throughout the country. They should know that a volcanic eruption can not be suppressed by firing rifles. Have the ministers any right to govern the country by rifles. .... The Government could not manage the show, because it was incompetent, because it was callous, characterless and corrupt."[7] The death of 80 agitators in the police firing shook the entire nation. Next day Ananda Bazar Patrika reported that "The police continued their operation till the late night in different parts of the central Calcutta. They chased the demonstrators, charged them with lathi, fired tear gas sells on them and arrested many of them. Pandemonium prevailed as street lights in this locality went off. Street lights were also put off in Cornwallis Street in North Calcutta and the police heavily patrolled in this area. We also learnt that in view of this tensed situation and also owing to attacks on vehicles, bus and tram services were closed, which caused great difficulties for the commuters from their office. The Government and most of the media observed that as the evening descended on the city, the hoodlums and anti-social element became active, which further deteriorated the situation."[8]

STUDENTS' PARTICIPATION

In this historic movement the revolutionary role of the students became obvious with their involvement to the movement. Calcutta witnessed enormous students' movement, violence and massacre that swept the streets of the city. After the incidents of 31st August, huge number of school and college students observed strike protesting the police action on that day. To protest against this incident, the students organized a rally on 1st September, 1959. A large number of College and University students participated in the rally. When the rally went towards Writers' Building, the police obstructed them and started tremendous lathi charge, used tear gas and even firing. Clearly, peaceful agitators were given chase by the police, making students fall in confusion. The students further pulled out hand-carts from sheds and use them as barricades to keep off police vehicles. A brief interval came in the trouble with heavy rainfall in the evening. But at the rain subsided, the disturbance resumed. Pitched battles took place near the Subodh Mallick Squire area. Panorama of disturbance soon shifted to the University Campus, College Street, where students responded to lathis and tear gas with bricks and other missiles. Near the University, the police had to move away for some time in the face of students' violent resistance. It was reported that turbans and batons of the police were snatched from them and then set on fire.[9] In this police recourse four students were killed and many more injured. Harinarayan Adhikary, the then prominent leftist student leader was seriously injured. The Durbhiksha Pratirodh Committee or the Famine resistance Committee staged dharna in different places of West Bengal against the police atrocities. The leaders who led the students in the Food Movement of 1959 were Gurudas Dasgupta, Tejarat Hussain, Aurobindo Ghosh, Sunil Sen, Pratul Lahiri and many others.[10]

It was noticed that the year 1959 saw five days of violent clashes between agitators and the state which, gave birth to three kinds of reaction[11]:

(1) an angry reaction against the government's handling of the situation;

(2) blaming the organizers of the movement for indulging in 'lawless anarchy';

(3) a balanced assessment which criticized both the government's food policy and its handling of the situation and the left leadership's losing control over the situation.

Before the sad memories of 1959 tapered of, came the year of 1960. Students of Calcutta University, Jadavpur University, Visva Bharati University, North Bengal University and almost all the Colleges of West Bengal began launching blockbuster movements on the issues which were related to their institutes and the prevailing educational system. As a matter of fact they combated against the situation. Students of school, too, came forward from different districts of West Bengal with a view to getting redress for their various problems through organizing movements and leading them to success. The crystallization of the grievances among the students began as per their assessment of the political condition of their state diverse activities on the basis of different political calculations started to gain militancy. And West Bengal came into limelight as a first class nursing home of indomitable student upheaval.[12]

INDO-CHINESE WAR AND THE STUDENTS

A quest for adding an international dimension to the thinking of the students of West Bengal in the background of Indo-Chinese confrontation started from this point. But unfortunately at this time the student movements got a stumbling block in course of its procession towards an expected goal. Deplorably as a consequence of this shock ultra nationalism in a frenzied attempt got the better of the progressive student force and side by side with it the Students Federation was declared anti-national and an illegal organization. The student community stood up with their full strength against this blind ultra nationalism. In support of it in different dailies of that time information and news on war were published to enlighten the students of that time about the excesses that were committed by the ultra nationalists. For example:

a) "To sit in a discussion with China India is always ready"–Nehru[13]

b) "China agrees to discuss frontier Problems"[14]

c) "India refuses the unconditional proposal of China"[15]

d) "Order has been given to drive away the infiltrators"–Nehru[16]

Students analyzed a bit deeply the main news in the 'Ananda Bazar Patrika' of 1962 and as a result they became doubtful about the truth of this news. They believed that this war was not being fought for saving the country from external aggression, but it was something else which seemed to them confusing. Supposedly students were conscious the truth underlined the mystery enshrouding the war reports. The National Council of the Communist Party of India branded China as aggressor and appealed to liberate farmers and ordinary people to stand by Nehru for the cause of their motherland. The rank and file of the Students Federation decided to go against the leadership of the students Federation.

In true sense of the term they rebelled against the leaders of the students Federation on this issue. The leaders in return called the rebels 'China Roaders'. Emergency was declared by the administration of the country for the whole national boundary. The leaders of the Congress Party like Nepal Roy, Atulya Ghosh and many others in different public gatherings commented, "Communists are antinational, cut asunder their hands and legs.[17] Some reports in 1962 of November and December published in Ananda Bazar Patrika increased the respect among the students about China.

> "The slogan of the Chinese soldiers in the snows of the Himalayas of brotherhood of the Indians and the Chinese".[18]

This information about China made the students more enthusiastic to know more about this country and beside this some reports again about the patriotism of the ruling class made them apprehensive of the veracity of its patriotic devotion. To quote Ananda Bazar Patrika–

> "Refusal of the students of schools to buy Red Pencil"[19]

The anti-Chinese sentiment increased and with it the College authorities became more inimical and they declared the Student Fedaration as illegal. Students who fought out peaceful resolution of all academic problems were out rightly expelled from their colleges. On the allegation of burning a picture of Nehru the students Union of Calcutta University was banned.[20]

The Indo-Chinese war influenced very deeply the sensibility of the students and their positive attitude. A storm of debate arose on such subject like war expansionism, imperialist economics and politics. Many conscious students began to be vociferous in saying that a socialist state cannot attack another country. They emphasized that aggression and imperialist designs on the territories of other countries are the inevitable result of imperialist economic exploitation. A sort of rift in the lute appeared in the movement of the two students' organization. One of these declared that the China was the aggressor country and another assured that the truth was exactly the opposite of it. At this time the apolitical students started slogan voicing that they wanted peace and not war, thus avoiding the debate over the role of China in the controversial Indo-Chinese showdown.[21] Posters began to show up in different Colleges and Universities of West Bengal containing such rhymes:

> "Jokhani prashna othei juddha na shanti
> Amader beche nite hainako bhranti
> Amra jabab dei, shanti, shanti, shanti".[22] (In Bengali)
>
> "Whenever question arises-peace or strife?
> Our reply, we want peace, peace and peace"
>
> (English Translation)

The Indo-Chinese war ended on the 20th November 1962 with the unilateral declaration of truce by China. As a result of this the force of the student movements suffered a setback.

After July, 1965, Student agitation started over the issue of hike of Tram and Bus fare. They picketed in the streets of Calcutta day after day and it acted as an inducement to the Tram Company employee strike for one single day against the said hike. This enthused the students to go forward tremendously. Students, as a token of their sincerity as protestors, boarded the Buses of different routes and requested passengers to refrain from paying escalated fares. A sort of stronghold unity developed among the passengers against the price hike. The passengers even began to resist the Tram and Bus Company to extort the increased rates of fare. Being faced with this reluctance from the side of the passengers the conductors too refrained from taking the increased fare. On the 3rd day of the movements i.e. 29th July 1965 order under the section 144 was promulgated in Calcutta. The police pounced upon the students with batons and teargas. Due to this repressive nature of the police action the student movement gradually became violent. Many students were wounded and many other arrested. Those who arrested were Azijul Hoque, Shyamal Chakraborty, Subhas Chakraborty, Asit Sinha, Shipra Bhowmik and so on. As a protest against these arrests the Left Parties called a bandh in Calcutta on 31st August 1965. The public unanimously responded to this call. The Calcutta University was declared for 3 days closure.[23]

INDO-PAK WAR AND THE STUDENTS

Indo-Pak war began with a bang at a time when the resistance movement against their escalation of fare gathered momentum. Taking the opportunity of India's being engaged in an international confrontation, the self seeking evil forces tried to foment communal riots in Calcutta and its adjoining areas. Being circumstanced thus political parties and students found it impossible to carry on with their programme of resisting any more fare hike. Now the principal duty of the student organization was to try hard to save communal harmony. Side by side with it anti war movement was also launched by the students. Both these seemingly were very tough tasks. In spite of this hassle the students Community of West Bengal came forward to help the Leftist student organizations to work together for keeping harmony among the various religious communities. On the other part of West Bengal, in the erstwhile East Pakistan, students started a pioneering movement against war and for establishing peace in their country on the basis of the principle of peaceful co-existence. In Calcutta too an impact of this movement was felt. The Leftist student organizations of Calcutta made their demand to end war even in the war time fluster through amicable settlement as much loud as possible for them. In the mean time public opinion of both the countries rose high and through a friendly intervention of the then Soviet Union, the Indo-Pak war ended at last. This military clash between the two countries triggered off a sort of a terrific economic crisis in this country[24] especially in West Bengal the tremendous food and fuel crisis. It was at this time students began pamphleting like this:

> "Whenever people want job and food
> In the frontier the bugle of begins to hoot"[25]

THE FOOD MOVEMENT OF 1966 AND THE STUDENTS

In the history of the Indian politics of the 1960s, the Food Movement of West Bengal of 1966 was a historic event. This historic Food Movement had socio-economic perspective. By utilizing different loopholes in the West Bengal Land Reforms Act, feudal lords began to keep their holding intact by way of deluding the government. The Land which was redundant remained fallow for longtime affecting total harvest. This meant that they had not to pay a huge amount of tax against the quantity of lands they owned. Along with this the rate of agricultural growth also began to go down. The Government used to levy a quantity of tax on the husking mills. But the owners of these mills did not pay these taxes.[26] According to Saibal Mitra, the student leader, the Food Movement took a tremendously violent turn because of the feudalistic agricultural politics of the congress led Government under the leadership of Prafulla Sen.[27] Apart from this, a huge quantity of rice continued to be illegally passed over to the erstwhile East Pakistan in collusion with the police. Apart from this subsequent to the Indo-Pak War the prices of the essential commodity shot up to go beyond the reach of ordinary buyers. For food and Kerosin Communist Party on the 30th January of 1966 called a massive gathering at the foot of the 'Sahid Minar'. A good number of students participated in this gathering to express their solidarity with the cause of the movement.[28]

In 1966, on 16th February, thousand of school student boys and girls alike expressed their grief over the dearth of rice and kerosene while standing before the office of the S. D. O. of the Basirhat Sub-division of North 24Parganas. Here they demanded continuous immediate supply of rice and kerosene oil at a cheap rate regularly without interruption. At first it was a spontaneous outburst of the people against inflation, price rise and curtailment of Civil Liberties. The police lathi charged on the aggrieved demonstrators and in this police action 6 students were wounded and 40 of them were arrested. After this incident the Food Movement spread throughout the district. It requires to be mentioned that the students demonstrated their protests against the police atrocities and the police in response fired upon them. In this firing Nurul Islam, a teenage student of the Tetulia Multipurpose School was gunned down. Nurul Islam became the first student martyr of the Food Movement of 1966.[29] With the killing of Nurul Islam the movement took a consolidated form where the districts became hotbeds of agitations, processions, demonstrations, blockade of roads and railways, destruction of electric polls, closure of schools etc. Dr. Basu opined that the intensity of the food movements changed the political complexion of the state. It not only ensured a steady decline in Congress support in the state but also became one of the factors that led to the split of the Communist Party of India. Prof. Marcus Franda, the US scholar also held the same opinion.[30]

Close on the heels of this incident Food Movement spread from South to the Northern part of West Bengal. In the North especially in the North Bengal University and its surroundings the students in great number took part in this Food Movement. In this movement participants were Kisan Chatterjee, Dilip Bagchi, Pabitra Pani Saha, Harisadhan Ghosh, Probodh Sarkar,

Ranjit Chattopadhyay, Ashok Nanda, Amit Sen, Kumkum Bhattacharyya and such others. In the view of Kisan Chatterjee, "The Food Movement was a student movement irrespective of their party and ideology and with the passage of days this student movement was gaining momentum". The agitators participating in this movement took out processions, arranged street meeting, sent deputations and etc. They ventilated their grief in this manner. Many teachers and students supported them and marched out in an apolitical line with them.[31]

As the news of the death of Nurul Islam reached at Naxalbari, a student demonstration took place at the Nanda Prasad High School premises under the leadership of Nathuram Biswas. Being astounded at seeing the spontaneous strike of the students the school authority expelled 6 students forthwith. This was definitely an undemocratic decision on the part of the school authority and to protest against it the students' community burst out in anger. A continuous strike was declared and began to be observed by the courageous students. Some of the residents of Naxalbari whole heartedly supported the student. To ensure uninterrupted study of the students who struck against, the authority arranged for them a makeshift school for their study. There were some educated persons of Naxalbari and scholar student of North Bengal University who used to teach the students. The name of Kisan Chatterjee, Dilip Bagchi, Pabitra Pani Saha are deserved to be mentioned. All of them played an indispensable role in the historic agrarian movement of Naxalbari.[32]

Large waves of countrywide demonstrations splashed upon such a premier seat of learning like Presidency College. Some courageous students came forward to give an integrated shape of an organization to the ill assorted student Front. One of the closely knit units of this student Front was made by one of the eminent leader like Asim Chatterjee of the Presidency College. Among his known associates and aides he was popularly known as 'Kaka' (uncle). A movement brewed in the Eden Hostel against various difficulties and autocratic attitude of the ruling class. After this, in 1966 in the Students' Union election, the organized Student Front came out with the thumping victory and won leadership. This consternated the education department of the Government. The authority of the Presidency College expelled 7 students of the undergraduate level and ordered not to admit another two demonstrators into the Post Graduate class. It is worth mentioning that those, against whom the punitive action was taken of, all active workers of the movement of the Hindu Hostel and members of the student union representing the Student Federation of the College.[33] In protest against this hostile attitude of the College authority a continuous sit-in strike started. This strike deadlocked the day to day functioning of the college and administrative set up. Day and night at the gate of the Presidency College a confluence of students coming from different colleges to express their whole hearted empathy with the demonstrating Presidency Collegians gave a new dimension to the militant demonstration. They chanted slogans and the slogans did not merely limit themselves to the demands of the demonstrating student of the Presidency College. Watch-words began to sound the demand of over all democratization of all the educational institutions. These demonstrating students even manifested their wish of uniting with the labour class in posters and in Party cries. A student of that time commented on this movement thus: "The movement has become an issue involving the entire student community and no longer one of establishing only their democratic rights."[34]

If it cannot be claimed that 100 percent support of the students of the Presidency College was in favour of this movement. At that time there was another student organization named P.C.S.O. in this college. It was always against this movement right from its inception. Skirmishes between this two student organizations broke out frequently in course of demonstration. The P.C.S.O was never in favour of an indefinite closure of the college which was otherwise whole heartedly demanded and supported by the opponents. Any way the P.C.S.O did not want to be troubled by raising the different demand by the Student Federation. The Statesman reported that, the students, loyal to the P.C.S.O started a signature campaign in which out of 1450 students of the Presidency College not less than 275 students put their signature.[35] The Statesman at this time published an article from which an extract is given here —

> "Its members are described today, in derision as opportunist and Pro-American. Rightly Perhaps, The organization is seen to mirror what is loosely termed the establishment. Its members, particularly the bulk of Presidency's 400 girls, are better off than the rest .....even the protest over the bombing of Hanoy and Haighphong was seen by many in the P.C.S.O as an ominous sign at the shape of things to come. They too join in the chorus of denunciation of unwarranted intrusions of politics into the sanctum of education".[36]

At the end of 1966 when the Food Movement of West Bengal became tremendously powerful, the state govt. sent a requisition to the Central Govt. for giving an immediate and effective check to it with repressive measures. The then Prime Minister Mrs. Indira Gandhi began parlance with the leftist leader detained in jail through emissary and then increased the per head allotment of food grains by 100 grams. In this way with the intervention of the Central Govt. the food movement came to an end. But the main problems, the crux of the issues, did not get any satisfactory solution. Almost all the demands remained unfulfilled. But curiously enough, hundreds of prisoner put behind the bars on political ground in connection with this movement, were released by the govt. and this the govt. did being compelled by the leaders of this protest movement. Students told that although the economic struggle did not evolved into a political struggle on the higher level, the govt. being impelled by the economic struggle might accept some of the political demands as legitimate. The proof of it was the freedom of the political prisoners. Here one thing should be made clear that during the Food Movement of 1966 among the 50 martyrs 28 were the students.[37]

According to Sugato Nandy 'The second Food Movement left over 40 dead in five days and several thousands were badly injured. Its political impact was tremendous. Senior Congress Minister, Ajoy Mukherjee resigned from Congress Party and formed Bangla Congress and made alliance with the Left Front to form the United Front in the election of 1967. The CPI and the newly formed Bangla Congress too called two separate food conventions on 6th March in Calcutta. But neither of the parties could persuade the masses to call off the movement. Thus, both the parties agreed to the peoples' demand and gave the call for a general strike for 24 hours on 10th March. But the spirit of popular spontaneity made the strike continue for another 24 hours'.[38]

SUMMING UP

From the above study, it is found that the students were very much concerned about the socio-economic problems of the country and even they were very conscious about the impact of the wars. The student participation in the food movements were spectacular as because they wanted food, not wars. Although, the Food Movement of West Bengal came to a temporary end, student movement was then widely seen all over India as a tremendously continuous process for reaching apparently to a definite goal.

NOTES AND REFERENCES

1. Dasgupta, H. and Adhikary, H. (1993 & 2008): Rajnaitik Poto Bhumite Bharitiya Upamahadesher Chhatra Andolan (in Bengali), Published by School for Peoples, Medinipore, and Radical Impression, Kolkata, p. 348.
2. Report of the Radhakrishnan Commission, 1949, Govt. of India, p.374.
3. Basu, S. P. (2012): Food Movements of 1959 and 1966, Seminar Proceedings titled "Popular Movements in West Bengal and Bihar", Dated. 28.02.2016, Kolkata, Found at *www.mcrg.ac.in* and also see Basu's article entitled "The Chronicle of a Forgotten Movement: 1959 Food Movement Revisited", 2012.
4. The Statesman, 27.04.1959.
5. The Statesman, 05.08.1959.
6. Ray, S. (2007): Marxist Parties of West Bengal (1947-2001), Progressive Publisher, Kolkata, pp-126-127.
7. Mukherjee, Biswanath's booklet "Khadya Sankater Janyo Daayi Ke ?" CPI Publication, Kolkata, 1969, p-19.
8. Ananda Bazar Patrika, 01.08.1959.
9. Amrita Bazar Patrika, 02.09.1959.
10. Dasgupta, H. and Adhikary, H. (1993 & 2008), pp. 186-187.
11. Basu, S. P. (2012): Food Movements of 1959 and 1966, Seminar Proceedings titled "Popular Movements in West Bengal and Bihar", Dated. 28.02.2016, Kolkata, Found at *www.mcrg.ac.in* and also see Basu's article entitled "The Chronicle of a Forgotten Movement: 1959 Food Movement Revisited", 2012.
12. Ibid. pp. 368-369.
13. Ananda Bazar Patrika, 02.10.1962.
14. ABP, 07.10.1962.
15. ABP, 08.10.1962.
16. ABP, 13.10.1962.

17. Acharya, A. (ed., 1998 & 2014): Shat-Sattarer Chhatra Andolan (in Bengali). An Article by Saibal Mitra, Anustup, Kol, and enlarged edition, pp.33-34.
18. ABP, 13.09.1962.
19. ABP, 20.09.1962.
20. Acharya, A. (ed., 1998 & 2014), p-34.
21. Acharya, A. (ed., 1998 & 2014), p.36.
22. Acharya, A. (ed., 1998 & 2014), p.40.
23. Acharya, A. (ed., 1998 & 2014), p.36.
24. Dasgupta, H. and Adhikary, H. (1993 & 2008), pp.452-453.
25. Acharya, A. (ed., 1998 & 2014), p.41.
26. Dasgupta, H. and Adhikary, H. (1993 & 2008), p.462.
27. Acharya, A. (ed., 1998 & 2014), p.48.
28. Dasgupta, H. and Adhikary, H.(1993 & 2008), p.462.
29. Ibid, p.463.
30. Basu, S. P. (2012), p. 3.
31. An Interview with Kisan Chatterjee, Dated. 22/01/2007.
32. An interview with Nathuram Biswas, Dated 05/01/2007.
33. Shat-Sattarer Chhatra Andolan, An Article by Subhash Ganguly, Anustup, Kol, 1998 p.157.
34. The Statesman, Dated. 11/11/1966.
35. Ibid, Dated. 10/11/1966.
36. The Statesman, Dated. 29.11.1966, an article entitled "Revolt in the College Street" by S. Datta Ray.
37. Shat-Sattarer Chhatra Andolan: An Article by Saibal Mitra, Anustup, Kol, 1998, & enlarged edition, 2014, p.52.
38. Nandy, Sugato: Events Violent, Moments Significant, E-Article, http:/mail.sarai.net/pipermail/reader-list/2007-March and also found in Basu's article entitled "The Chronicle of a Forgotten Movement: 1959 Food Movement Revisited", 2012, p. 17.

6

Involvement of Students in the Naxalbari Peasant Uprising and After (1967-1977)

In 1967, the outbreak of an agrarian movement at Naxalbari, in the outskirts of the Siliguri Sub-division of Darjeeling district, was an event of great significance not only in the history of the agrarian movements but also in the subsequent movements also. The name 'Naxalbari' is now a well-known place in the political atlas in India. The peasants of this area protested against the age long Jotedars' domination. One significant feature of the movement was the participation of students in the movement at par with peasants. But till now, their role was not highlighted by any scholar or historian. In this chapter, a humble attempt is made to highlight and locate the role of students in the Naxalbari Peasant Movement.

NEW DIMENSION OF STUDENT MOVEMENT

During this time the student movement broke away from the vestige of its past and took a new line of operation. At first it denied any stewardship of any political party. In fact, it grew into an indomitable off spring of the society. This was an age of marvelously new age of protest and rational opposition to anything conventional.[1] One can mark this time as one of acceptance of any argument with cautious examination of its truth. In the 19th Century Bengal Renaissance Derozio gave leadership to a vibrant Young Bengal. The achievement of such a scale cannot stand up right by the age rational opposition, which we have already referred to. In brief, the youth of the then Bengal was a bold and fourth right man. This man was irritated too much by the adverse situation of his time and endeavoured to raise himself to the highest height, which was more than his in born greatness. These are the circumstances, which explain very clearly this youth's sense of revolution. Often the sensibilities of this youth would explode violently if his individualism and sense of right were interfered with.[2]

However, from what has been discussed above it must not be concluded that every youth of that times Bengal was like others. In fact, it was just an idealization of a young man who devoted himself to revolutionize and otherwise outdated social system. But here too a risk of over simplification of a social phenomenon runs in this act of idealization. Statistically in the student and youth movement, the active participation of the students and youth was to the turn of twenty to twenty five percent. But this movement could be as powerful as many others provided it with unquestioning support. Already a reference has been made to the explosion of anger of students but that was a mixture of socio-economic and political reactions. This was the witch's brew of every movement.[3]

In the year 1967, when student movement reached its climax the 4th General Election was held. Along with this election, Assembly Polls in some of the states of India were also conducted. West Bengal was one of these states. People's grief became terrific at this time and demonstrations started to manifest people's disapproval of the attitudes of the National Congress Party, the then all India ruling party. Disintegration in the Congress party was seen. With this background the leftists in West Bengal started their preparation with full force for the election, which was announced to be held in the month of February, 1967.[4] On the eve of the election of 1967, CPI(M) promised in their Election Manifesto that they would end the police interference in stopping any democratic movement, if they were ever brought into power.[5] Seeing that the promise which made by the Left Front, the leftist students began an extensive publicity campaign in support of them. After the election, it was found that the leftist had won the battle for power and as a consequence 14 Party United Front Government was formed. West Bengal got Mr. Ajoy Mukherjee, the leader of Bangla Congress as the Chief Minister of the United Front Government.[6]

LOOKING AT NAXALBARI

In the Assembly Polls of 1967, Jangal Santal of CPI (M) was chosen as a candidate from the Naxalbari Assembly Seat. His supporters of Naxalbari and the students of North Bengal University in a body campaigned for him. Nathuram Biswas, the then student leader of Naxalbari area said, "We campaigned widely in support of Jangal Santal and against Government, police and jotedars. We participated in different meetings and processions. To side with us some students from NBU took part in this publicity drive. In spite of this intensive and extensive campaigning, Jangal Santal courted defeat in that election by a margin of 4000 votes. Ishwar Tirki, a candidate of congress won the poll. Jangal Santal might have failed in the contest but we did not lose heart because Left Front in West Bengal achieved victory and United Front Government was established under the leadership of Mr. Ajay Mukherjee. We believed that, henceforth, all our problems would be solved, atrocities usually committed by jotedars and the police would come to an end. But within a few days things began to take a reverse direction to frustrate us."[7] Kisan Chatterjee, veteran Student Leader of 60s, NBU, of this time held the same view. He said, "In 1967 election, we continued our campaign at Naxalbari and Siliguri for the Left Front. Being satisfied by the election promises offered by the CPI(M) and keeping in our mind the evil of the bad administration of the Congress Party. We, especially Dilip Bagchi, Pabitra Pani Saha, Kumkum Bhattacharyya, Ranjit Chatterjee, Probodh Sarkar and Amit Sen took part in the election campaign. But the victory of the Left Front did not bring about any changes in the hitherto repulsive political landscape of west Bengal. This was a starter of the jingoist movement of the students who were then much agonized by the frustrating volte-face of the Left front Government."[8]

In the March of 1967, after a few days of the oath taking ceremony for the Left front Ministry, the victorious MLA as well as a big land owner Ishwar Tirki beat Begul Kisan, a bargadar (share-cropper) in his farm for uprooting him from his homestead. When the Peasant Association of Naxalbari protested against this conspiracy Ishwar Tirki struck out his gun. At this, the peasants went to the police and complained them of this incident. The police in response went to the area of violence not to arrest Ishwar Tirki but to nab the member of the victimized Peasant Association. The adverse impact of this incident was reflected in the behaviour of the peasants and students. The students went in a procession demanding the immediate arrest of Ishwar Tirki without blinking at his crime.[9] It can be said that this was the background of the armed peasant uprising that took place at Naxalbari.

On 18th March 1967, at Rambola Jote of Naxalbari a convention of peasants was held. In this convention the decision of launching armed struggle against Government, Police and Jotedars was taken. On the 7th May same year at Bandarjhuli of Naxalbari area divided all the land holding among the peasants and handed over all powers of administering these lands to them. It was decided that the police would not be allowed to enter the villages. All the weapons of the jotedars would have to be seized and with them the peasants would have to be armed. Above all, as that decision said, all sale deeds of all lands would have to be gutted.[10] Some students of NBU and the students residing at Naxalbari supported this decision of the Peasants' Association. From a statement made by Kisan Chatterjee, it came to be known that a band of students of NBU went to different villages of Naxalbari to bring out paddy and rice from the houses of jotedars for distributing among the needy peasants under the leadership of Kisan Chatterjee, Dilip Bagchi and Pabitra Pani Saha.[11]

The incidents of 24th and 25th May of 1967 rocked the whole world. Till today the circumstances that led to this incident and the incidents themselves are a mystery to many of us. On the 24th May 1967, a big detachment of the police entered the villages of Naxalbari to resist the peasants from carrying on with their armed looting and plundering. The police had at that time an additional responsibility to save the jotedars too. Hundreds of armed peasant attacked the police with bows & arrows, stick and lances. They killed a police named Sonam Wangdi on the spot. Another police officer Mr. Narayan Chakraborty was pierced by a number of arrows and being wounded thus he began shouting, "save me, save me". Seeing that the situation was taking an untoward direction other policemen got back. But the next day i.e. 25th May, a number of policemen and Para-military forces made forays into these villages killed indiscriminately 11 persons. Among these 11 persons 9 were women, a child and a farmer.[12] Later, after a survey and an interview with Khokan Majumdar the name of eight women and one peasant could be known who were killed in police firing. The names of the persons killed in this incident were identified as Dhaneswari Devi, Phulmati Devi, Goudrou Shaibani, Simaswari Mallick, Nayenswari Mallick, Sonamati Singh, Surabala Barman, Shyamaswari Shaibani and Kharsingh Mallick. Thereafter, Naxalbari High School police camp of different kinds was posted against any such armed insurgency. Not only at the Naxalbari High School, but also in rural areas and tea gardens police camps started working to the same effect. Inevitably, the rebel peasants went into the hideouts and from there they continued to direct their followers in their struggle against the Government atrocities. During this time youths and students of Naxalbari carried information about the rural peasants to different hideouts and vice-versa.[13]

After this peasant uprising of Naxalbari a big section of youths and students community began deliberating on revolutionary politics and even some of them plunged into the activities to contribute to the revolution for the emancipation of the peasants and labourers.[14] It seems that the Naxalbari struggle created a stir among the students of North Bengal University and Presidency College who organized demonstration in support of the peasant struggle.[15] According to Kisan Chatterjee, the then veteran student leader of NBU, the problems of the peasant always posed to be social problem to them. They claimed that they were aware the demands and the aspirations of the peasants much ahead of the day when the Naxalbari uprising occurred. Many students regularly attended different meetings and assemblies of the peasants. That is why they considered the peasants' want and aspirations as social problem.[16] While explaining the reason that drove Naxalbari to the peasant upheaval Kisan Chatterjee enlightened us about the background of the students' participation in the movement: "80% of the students of the whole of West Bengal come from the families of the peasants and workers. Therefore, these students are well aware of the day to day problems that plunged the peasants and workers. This made us to believe that the problems of the peasants of Naxalbari were the problems of our society as a whole. So, we did not hesitate in jumping into the movement irrespective of our party loyalty and ideological belief."[17]

After the Naxalbari uprising the Government appointed a few loyal informers for tracing the Naxalites, hiding in the rural areas. Taking the help of these informers the police combed the villages and perpetrated atrocities in the houses of few peasants. Even the women of this place were not spared. This torture continued time and again. When the news of this torture reached NBU, about 70% of the students of the University began to protest these police excesses. They decided that they would stop the police vehicle at Shibmandir area near NBU. As per this decision about 50-60 students of NBU in the middle of June in one morning stopped three to four police Jeep coming from Naxalbari. The Jeeps were carrying a few peasant arrested at Naxalbari. There were some informers in these Jeeps who used to help the police in arresting the peasants. The news of the intersection of the police jeeps went to the Hostel of NBU and near about 300 students reached Shibmandir areas which strengthened the students' assemblies. They started beating the police without any let-up or hindrance and then snatched away the arrested peasant from the police custody. Immediately, the SDO of Siliguri Sub-Division arrived at the place of incident and to him a demand for an unconditional release of the prisoners was placed. The SDO ordered a release of the arrested peasants after understanding the seriousness of the situation. One thing deserved to be mentioned here is that the students snatched away the informers from the police Jeeps, shaved their heads, putting around their necks wreaths of shoes and they were made to walk in the streets of Shibmandir.[18] This was a manifestation of the fume of grief accumulated among the students of NBU for a long time.

Immediately, after this incident three students were suspended from attending the class by the University Authority on charge of intercepting police vehicle and snatching away prisoners. They were also accused of forcefully taking away food grains from the house of Jotedars. These three student leaders were Kisan Chatterjee, Dilip Bagchi and Pabitra Pani Saha. Students started a big rally against the suspension order of the University. This movement gradually spread throughout West Bengal. The agitating students placed a charter of demands before starting their movements. The demands were:

1. Immediate withdrawal of the suspension order served upon Kisan Chatterjee, Dilip Bagchi and Pabitra Pani Saha.

2. Withdrawal of the security force and the police by declaring the emergency as null and void.
3. Immediate holding of examinations after restoration of peaceful and normal condition in the University without any delay.
4. Nullifying all cases against the students and withdrawal of arrest warrant against them.

After these demands were placed by the agitating students, Prof. A. C. Roy, the then Vice-Chancellor, NBU arranged a convention. But the agitators boycotted the convention and clearly opined that the day to day administration of the University could not be continued only with the help of police and military.[19]

Close on the heels of the snatching of the imprisoned peasants from the police custody by the students of NBU, the students were suffering from police atrocities and anti-social repression. After the snatching was committed, anti-socials of Siliguri were set on the students. The supporters and leaders of Naxalbari movement dwelling Siliguri appraised the students of NBU of these atrocities. These made the students of NBU very alert about the reality of the situation[20]. In the month of 1967, one day at noon a band of armed miscreants came outside, a Truck entered in the University and began searching for the pro-Naxalbari students. The news of this eventuality reached the Hostel and massive number of students came out armed with sticks and clubs. They encircled the miscreants and beat them black and blue. Noticing that the situation was going out of control, the NBU authority called off the police and Para-military forces in the University campus and closed the Hostels, postponed all the examinations sine die. Prof. A. C. Roy, the then Vice-Chancellor issued an order to the students to vacate the Hostels instantaneously. The agitators left the Hostels and went home.[21]

Although, the agitators went home, the movement did not stop completely. On 22nd September, 1967 Kisan Chatterjee was arrested at Suri of Birbhum District and this triggered of a fresh demonstration, which spread throughout West Bengal. At noon of 30th September, 1967 students of different localities of Calcutta assembled at the University of Calcutta and in protest against the arrest of Kisan Chatterjee. A long procession of the students marched towards the Writers' Building. When it reached to Esplanade (East), was obstructed by a police cordon. Four representatives from this procession of students met the Hon'ble Education Minister and submitted to him a deputation. Speeches by different student leaders like Dilip Bagchi, Saibal Mitra, Ajijul Haque were delivered before this cordon procession. In the speeches protest was sounded against the arrest of Kisan Chatterjee and other students. The speakers demanded their release from jail and the acquittal of Jangal Santal and other peasants, arrested in connection with the Naxalbari movement.[22]

MOVEMENT SHIFTED FROM NORTH TO SOUTH

A tremendous reaction among the students of Calcutta and its adjoining areas was seen after the incidents involving Naxalbari areas of 24th & 25th of May, 1967. Thereafter, Students' Federation led by CPI (M) faced with disintegration into two belligerent fractions. The fraction led by Dinesh Majumdar began propagating for CPI (M) which was a party to the Naxalbari Movement among the students. On the other hand, Saibal Mitra, Asim Chatterjee, Dilip Pain, Santosh Rana sided with the armed peasant struggle of Naxalbari.[23] The latter group, after the day of Naxalbari uprising started sticking posters on the walls of different colleges including the Presidency College and the University of Calcutta in support of the revolutionary peasants. Here, mention must be made of the fact that the posters were posted in the name of Students' Federation.[24]

In 1967, on 24th June a convention was held in the Rammohan Library Hall of Calcutta in support of the armed peasant struggle of Naxalbari. The group which was carrying on with this political works remaining within the CPI (M) was the organizers of this convention. In this convention 'Naxalbari Peasant Struggle Assistance Association' was formed. The students who were moved by the spell of the Naxalbari movement were mostly the leaders and supporters of CPI (M).[25] These students improvised a revolution which could change their society with the romantic enthusiasm of the youth. The Chinese Communist Party analyzed this movement and told that they were the 'Resounding Thunder of Spring'.[26] With thunderous clamours the students of North Bengal and Calcutta rose up to the occasion.

In view of the series of incidents that took place in Naxalbari in the name of the peasant struggle purging of the Naxalbari path began in the West Bengal Unit of the CPI (M). Within 1967 many party members were expelled from the levels of State Committee, District Committees and Local Committees. Among those expelled were Charu Majumdar, Saroj Dutta, Sushital Roychaudhury, Souren Bose, Kanu Sanyal and many others. Mainly, at the initiative of all these expelled party leaders the 'All India Co-Ordination Committee of Revolution' (AICCR) was formed on 13th November 1967. These expelled leaders began publishing 'Deshabrati', a Bengali weekly and 'Liberation', English Monthly. The news of the publication of these two news papers the supporters of Naxalbari movement and innumerable students and youth felt deeply influenced. These two news papers had an identical and ideological stand with the 'Chhatra Fauj' which was published by the radical students.[27]

Following the occurrence of the peasant struggle of Naxalbari, revolutionary functionaries among students got separated into two different parts. These two fractions were

Chhatra Fauj and Presidency Consolidation respectively. Almost, all Colleges of Calcutta and Jadavpur got themselves entangled with any of these fractions. They looked upon the Naxalbari peasant struggle as a peoples' liberation war of India. The Chinese Communist Party particularly came out with full support for the Naxalbari peasant struggle. These acted as a fantastic inspiration to the radical students. The aim of the students was to destroy the sources and the roots of rural feudal exploitation. Side by side with it they wanted to uproot the roots of imperialism from different levels of the society in India.[28]

On the issue of supporting the Naxalbari peasant movement, Chhatra Fauj and Presidency Consolidation were involved in a severe mutual internecine battle. One can get a proof of this battle of opinion from an article, anonymously written and published in Deshabrati. This anonymous writer of the article sent out a call, said, "Friends, petty bourgeois, petty Trotskyites bourgeois and jingoist economists have become very active in different spheres of life. They do not organize a student on the basis of the politics of agrarian revolution. They are misleading the students by making them party to movement for achieving the fulfillment of limited demands. They are engaging the students in making political propaganda works and forming organization to start movement for highlighting very trivial issues. They are reactionaries and revisionists. Comrade starts struggle against these political opportunists".[29] This letter published in Deshabrati was mainly a focus on the belligerence of the Presidency Consolidation and Chhatra Fauj with each other. Although, the two fractions were torn by political conflicts between them, the events of Naxalbari cast on indelible spell over them.

In reality the Naxalbari incident was never an expression of simple version of theoretical and imaginary programme of action. The students actually found in it a living and realistic schedule of action against the cruel reactionary forces of India.

Social transformation was not merely a word of books- this stood out as an outstanding truth in Russia and China. India, along with these countries was a fertile ground for starting this transformation as an irrefutable support to this claim of the revolutionaries. The Naxalbari uprising is always offered as a proof of this.[30] But leftist students were disarranged by the Naxalbari phenomenon. Fractional differences bungled the ideological unity among them. In 1967, the fact that came out as a stark truth was that Communist Students' Federation were faced with a three part division- one part of it was led by CPI, another by CPI(M) and last but not the least the followers of the Naxalbari peasant struggle i.e. the Radical Students' Federation.[31]

Right at the start of 1968 going along the part of Naxalbari began to gain strength by degrees. The students were gaining strength spontaneously, although, they did not have any central organization. In many of the colleges of West Bengal a storm started to rage very easily. At the beginning of 1968 in the election that was held at Bangabasi College Students' Federation inspired by neo-fangled politics occupied 60 seats out of 68. The opposition students' wing was the Chhatra Parisad led by Subrata Mukherjee which was pitted against the Students' Federation. This victory in the Students Union election at Scottish Church College and City Commerce College created as sensation in the College Street locality.[32] Everywhere in West Bengal Naxalite Students could strengthen their bases and this was proved by a report published in the Ananda Bazar Patrika. From that report of 9th March 1968, it could be known at that time an official survey was undertaken. This survey revealed that in 65 colleges of the state the Naxalite candidates won in the Students' Union election.[33]

Students supporting path of action raised various political issues in the above said elections. These were global movement against imperialistic exploitation, comparative study of the roles played by China and Soviet Union in different national liberation movement, Vietnamese liberation war, the revolutionary way of China, the agrarian revolution spreading in India, Naxalbari phenomena and that of the first United Front Government of West Bengal to name a few. On the basis of these political issues the foundation was made for fortifying the stand of the Naxalbari path.[34] In fact, after the Naxalbari uprising the students wanted to highlight their revolutionary profile for liberating the oppressed classes of the state.[35]

HOW FAR THE STUDENTS CONSCIOUS?

How far student community was conscious about the social realities can be ascertained by dividing it into three parts. First of these three parts is the political consciousness and this part is very well organized and usually led the students' demonstration. To the second part belonged a group of active workers who usually works keeping the leadership at the centre. Some of these workers were conscious, some less conscious and still others were there who usually took part in different students' movements on account of either on the ground of humanity or democracy. In almost all the students' organizations these democrats and humanists were usually account for large number. The third part of the student community was a mammoth crowd of students who never supported any organization but jumped into action whenever these movements gained maximum momentum. They came like powerful cascades and they recede whenever they look the adequate stimulation for doing it. This is the usual picture of the political behavior of the student community as a whole. But when Naxalbari came into relief as a spot of revolutionary rebellion the intra-community could not any more disturb the students in uniting very strongly for the cause of representing very stubbornly the oppressed classes of their society. A large scale political and social awakening took place in the psychology of the students of West Bengal. This was proved clearly when in 1968 Dharmveer, the then Governor of West Bengal advised the dismantling of the United Front Cabinet. Then it was the radical students who protested very hardly against this decision of the Governor, whatever might be the reason of the fall of the United Front Government, the way of suspending the Government was not at all taken lightly by the radicals. Loud and severe protest was made by the radicals against these showdowns by the Government.[36]

In 1968 on 20th February, the Cabinet of Dr. Prafulla Ghosh was rendered inactive by an official directive. President's Rule came in the wake of it. It lasted for one year in West Bengal. During this time the supporters of Naxalbari movement became the victim of police atrocities. At this time many of the Naxalite workers and leaders were arrested and the rest went into hideouts. Mid- term poll fixed on the date of 9th February, 1969 came with a bang. Election was held and the United Front came out with absolute majority. The second United Front Government was formed. Within a few days of the formation of this Government, a bloody conflict took place between the youth of CPI(M) and the radical students. In this conflict, a worker of DYFI, Krishna Roy by name died. Excitement spread in the College Street area after the death of Krishna Roy. Thus, began a protracted conflict between the two groups, which is still continued.[37]

FORMATION OF RADICAL STUDENT WING

Another historic event occurred following the path of Naxalbari politics in the days of Second United Front Government. On 22nd April of 1969, on the birth day of Lenin in Calcutta in a secret meeting of AICCR the Communist Party of India (Marxist-Leninist) or CPI(M-L) was constructed. In a public meeting on 1st day of May, 1969 at the foot of Sahid Minar Comrade Kanu Sanyal, one of the eminent Naxal leaders announced the formation of such a party. On the day of announcement of CPI (M-L) the presence of radical students and youth was impressive.[38]

After the announcement of the formation of the CPI(M-L) the radical students and youth worker keeping the political directives of the RYSF high above participated freely in putting the political programme of action of the CPI(M-L) into reality. Students, supporters of Naxalbari path of action, were attracted by the activities of the Communist Party of China. They propagated the message and the spirit of the Redbook and the philosophy of Mao-Tse-Tung. They began sloganeering, as 'the chairman of China is our Chairman'. The radical students left cities for villages to work hand in hand with the peasants there. They sacrificed themselves in making a stronghold of peasant movement in the rural areas of West Bengal. A struggle for political emancipation started in the country thereby necessitating collection of small weapons, organizing secret association and making safe hideouts. They started movements against the ruling class for saving the peasants from the tortures of jotedars. If needed, they even took resort to politics of man haunting. Thus, in 1969 during the regime of the United Front Government the deliberation of the radical students and youth and their activities began to surface day after day in the different parts of the state especially in Calcutta, 24 Parganas, Midnapore, Birbhum, and Siliguri.[39]

SPREAD OF THE MOVEMENT

The spread of the Naxalbari Movement and its violent character panicked the Congress Government at the centre, and the United Front Government in the state. The fears of the two Governments were mainly due to the revolutionary outcry of the Naxalite students. They called the supporters of Naxalite movement to take part in the campaign of 'Let's move to the villages'. In this campaign several skirmishes between the hooligans of the jotedars and the Naxalites, three persons were killed. A proof in support of this incident can be found in the issue of Ananda Bazar Patrika of 7th May, 1969. The report reads like this: "Sudeb, Sashi and Gurudas were killed in the hands of the goondas of Jotedars at Keshpur Police Station. Among these three persons Sudeb Chakraborty was a student and the rest two were peasants." In Calcutta too the radical students clashed with their opponents. This made the Govt. anxious. Following this incident, in the Rajja Sabha, the Union Home Minister appealed, "all to unite against the Naxalite'.[40] In West Bengal Mr. Jyoti Basu, the then Deputy Chief Minister of the United front Government, remarked that, "the Naxalites were half political and half antisocial elements".[41] In a rally in the Maidan of Calcutta Mr. Promod Dasgupta, the then prominent leader of the CPI(M) told that, "if the police handed over to them the Naxalites, they would given them the proper dressing down within a matter of 24 hours." He went further to wonder, "whether the guns of the policemen were jammed with condoms, otherwise how came it that the Naxalites did not die of bullet injury."[42] In a straighten reply to this brazen reactionary stand of the CPI(M), Mr. Kanu Sanyal asserted that, "they would counter to violence with violence."[43] In this way the whole perspective of move to village campaign was turned into a theatre of armed encounters, murders and police repressions.

Mr. Charu Majumdar, the main organizer and the first secretary of the CPI (M-L), in the continuing circumstances wrote an article which featured a call to the students and youth. An extract of this article published in Deshabrati "....in every stage of the national movement of India youth and student of Bengal sacrificed all their personal interest selflessly. They made the message of liberation and the struggle for it reach village after village undauntedly. They tackled bravely the policy of the repression of the police. They kept themselves busy day in and day out for working as political ideologues after ending violently the 'dream of making career' though being studious scholars. In this time when a new age is coming into being when the imperialism is about to face complete destruction, when in countries all over the world revolution blazing to daunt the reactionaries, when the revolutionary fire has spread from Naxalbari to Srikakulam, from Assam to the Punjab, then this self sacrificing students and youths of Bengal should take over the responsibility of propagating revolutionary politics among the labourers and peasants. They must be attentive to the case of impoverish and landless peasants in this regard."[44] On the 5th March of 1970, in another article published in Deshabrati, Charu Majumdar addressed the students, "Now leave your schools and colleges and begin pursuing the end of revolutionary by all means."[45] After reading all these articles radical students began engaging themselves in various destructive activities.

With the call that Charu Majumdar blared to the students and youths demonstration of their grief began to take place here and there increasingly. They involved themselves in different thrilling adventures. They started to destroy the icons, burning libraries, destroying regularly different educational institutions. They even infiltrated M.M.G. led by Ananta Singh in order to commit dacoity in various banks for realizing political aim.[46] They did not spare such high profile national heroes like Gandhi-Subhash-Rabindranath and like. Their busts were broken and pictures sullied.[47]

AFTER NAXALBARI AND THE STUDENTS

In this background of the politics of West Bengal in the beginning of the decade of 1970s it became clear that the trend of the politics of the 60s has begun to turn to something new. The tidal waves of the student movement started by the radicals began to suffer waning. They began to differ openly. The CPI (M-L) theoreticians like Sushital Roychaudhury and Asit Sen publicly decried the politics of the radical students and youth attacking educational institutions and violent haunting of acclaimed social and political leaders. The revolutionary path taken by the radical students ran directly counter applied Naxalism. The disintegration of the CPI(M-L) foreboded an expected disintegration in the radical student movement. The wrong politics of the CPI (M-L) stifled the protest movement of the radical students.[48]

An evaluation of the performance of the Naxalite students of this time the party organ of the SFI said, "To put this nefarious plan of the Congress to action educational institutions have been chosen as places for putting its forces on display. These forces used 1200 Naxalites to launch attack on the revolutionaries. From 1970 to 1971, the authorities of 250 schools announced closure of them for a few days to stop implementation of these measures. Some workers and leaders of BPSF were murdered. Teachers, Professors and even the Vice-Chancellor of Jadavpur University were became the victims of this politics of assassination. Prof. Gopal Sen, the then Vice-Chancellor of Jadavpur University was killed because he wanted to hold examinations and withdrew CRPF from the campus of it. Bimal Das, the then Head Master of Durgapur High School was tied to a chair and then burnt up. Prasanta Sarkar, the then joint secretary of BPSF, Nadia District, was put to death while he was going to take his examination. Thus, began a series of murders daily."[49]

In the first part of the 1970s it became clear that the intensity of the student movement was dying down. The pioneers including the numberless youth and students began working for bringing a radical change in the political system of the country in the second half of the 1960s. The failure in the organization of the revolutionary programme frustrated these pioneers. For this the radical students and youths beat a tragic retreat. In the first half of the year 1971 after the

Bangladesh Liberation War, a vacuum in the political scene of West Bengal became conspicuous because of the backing out of the radical students from the path of democratic movement. The said vacuum was inevitably filled up by the SFI and Chhatra Parishad, ostensibly the self-seekers. This makes it clear that the terrorist activities of the radical students could not get any favourable support from the society. It was a tactical failure. Not only in India, but also in America and Europe the high waves of the radical students' movement were gradually receding back to non-entity. The armed adventures of the youth and students of Srilanka fizzled out after the Government there trembled for a time, which was a result of violent shake off done by the rebels.[50]

During this time economic crisis rocked the people tremendously, caused by slackening production, rising prices and growing unemployment. In West Bengal, the economy was virtually drifting into chaos from 1972-1973. Acute shortage of power led to loss of production from 1973-1974. Assistance from the Union Government towards meeting the grim situation of West Bengal was extremely inadequate. Even the then Chief Minister of the State was expressing his dissatisfaction with the Union Government for not complying with the request of the state for larger resources in the Fourth Five Year Plan. At this time a strong student and youth movement sprang up against rising prices, food shortage, high unemployment and Government corruption.[51] Meanwhile, in 1974 the BPSF and SFI organized a Conference with the demand for low-cost paper, kerosene and free Madhyamik education. A huge number of college and university students attended the conference.[52]

SUMMING UP

Therefore, it is true that the students being stimulated by the Naxalbari flare up could realize the importance of the necessity of attending to the problems of the peasants. They repeatedly proposed to occupy the position of power through armed struggle. But their idea about the problems of the peasants and the armed struggle for removing them was not clear. So, the leftist movement deviated from the Naxalbari path of action and degenerated terroristic aggression of the CPI (M-L). Not only that, the demonstrating youth and students began to be refused by the glowing of the Naxalite way of politics and the new terroristic belligerence.[53] In fact, the exuberance in their endeavour to topple the existing system of the idealist revolutionaries in understanding where laid the differences between the euphoric Naxalism and Neo-terrorism.

NOTES AND REFERENCES

1. Acharya, A. (ed., 1998 & 2014): Shat-Sattarer Chhatra Andolan (in Bengali), An Article by Ranabir Samaddar, Anustup, Kolkata, & Enlarged Edition, p. 138.
2. Banerjee, S.(1980): In the Wake of Naxalbari, Subarnarekha, Kolkata, pp. 64-66.
3. Acharya, A. (ed., 1998 & 2014), p. 140.
4. Dasgupta, H. and Adhikary, H. (1993 & 2008): Rajnaitik Poto Bhumite Bharatiya Upamahadesher Chhatra Andolan(In Bengali), School for People, Medinipore, and Radical Impression, Kolkata, p. 482.
5. An Interview with Khokan Majumdar, Extremist Peasant Leader, Naxalbari, Dated. 05.01.2007.
6. Dasgupta, H. and Adhikary, H. (1993 & 2008), pp. 482-483.
7. An Interview with Nathuram Biswas, Student Leader of 1960s, Dated. 05.01.2007.
8. An Interview with Kishan Chatterjee, Veteran Student Leader of 1960s, NBU, Dated. 22.01.2007.
9. An Interview with Nathuram Biswas, Student Leader of 1960s, Dated. 05.01.2007.
10. Majumdar, K. (2004): Naxalbari: Bharater Booke Basanter Vajranirghos (in Bengali), Siliguri, pp. 24-25.

11. An Interview with Kishan Chatterjee, Veteran Student Leader of 1960s, NBU, Dated. 22.01.2007.

12. An Interview with Khokan Majumdar, Extremist Peasant Leader, Naxalbari, Dated. 05.01.2007 & Pain Swapan Kumar's article on *Women in the Naxalbari Uprising: A Historical Overview*, published in the Journal of Indian History, Vol. LXXXVI, parts. 1-3, 2007, Department of History, University of Kerala, p. 280.

13. Majumdar, K. (2004): Naxalbari: Bharater Booke Basanter Vajranirghos, An Article by Nathuram Biswas on Student Movement, Siliguri, p. 92.

14. Dakshin Desh, 21st June, 1968.

15. Sen, S. (1982): Peasant Movement in India in the 19th & 20th Centuries, Kolkata, p.219.

16. An Interview with Kishan Chatterjee, Veteran Student Leader of 1960s, NBU, Dated. 22.01.2007.

17. Ibid.

18. Ibid.

19. Dakshin Desh, 4th December, 1967.

20. An Interview with Kishan Chatterjee, Veteran Student Leader of 1960s, NBU, Dated. 22.01.2007.

21. Deshabrati, Dated. 14th September, 1967.

22. Dakshin Desh, 7th October, 1967.

23. Dasgupta, H. and Adhikary, H. (1993 & 2008), p. 485.

24. Acharya, A. (ed., 1998 & 2014): Shat-Sattarer Chhatra Andolan, An Article by Saibal Mitra, published by Anustup, Kolkata, & Enlarged Edition, p. 61.

25. Dasgupta, H. and Adhikary, H.(1993 & 2008), p. 485.

26. Dasgupta, H. and Adhikary, H.(1993 & 2008), p. 486. The Party Organ of the Chinese Communist Party *Peking Review* of the 12th July of 1968 published an Article under the heading of *The Historic Turn in the Indian Revolution.* In this Article the phrase *Resounding Thunder of Spring* was used.

27. Dasgupta, H. and Adhikary, H. (1993 & 2008), p. 490.
28. Dasgupta, H. and Adhikary, H. (1993 & 2008), p. 491.
29. Deshabrati, Dated. 28th March, 1968, p. 12.
30. Acharya, A. (ed., 1998 & 2014), p. 69.
31. Dasgupta, H. and Adhikary, H.(1993 & 2008), p. 488.
32. Shat Dashaker Biplabi Chhatra Andolan, Magazine, 1968, p. 24.
33. Ananda Bazar Patrika, 9th May, 1968.
34. Dasgupta, H. and Adhikary, H. (1993 & 2008), p. 493.
35. Acharya, A. (ed., 1998 & 2014), p. 69 .
36. Acharya, A. (ed., 1998 & 2014), pp. 69-70 .
37. Acharya, A. (ed., 1998 & 2014): Shat-Sattarer Chhatra Andolan, An Article by Ranabir Samaddar, p. 497.
38. Banerjee, S. (1980), pp. 170-171.
39. Acharya, A. (ed., 1998 & 2014), p. 501.
40. Ananda Bazar Patrika, 7th May, 1969.
41. Ibid. p. 73.
42. Dasgupta, H. and Adhikary, H.(1993 & 2008), p. 71.
43. Ibid. p. 73.
44. Deshabrati, Dated. 29th August, 1969.
45. Ibid. Dated. 5th March, 1970.
46. Acharya, A. (ed., 1998 & 2014), p. 73.
47. Acharya, A. (ed., 1998 & 2014), p. 145.
48. Dasgupta, H. and Adhikary, H. (1993 & 2008), p. 509.
49. Sangothito Chhatra Andolaner Panchas Bacharer Aitijya O Uttaradhikar, published by SFI, West Bengal State Committee, 1971, p. 68.
50. Acharya, A. (ed., 1998 & 2014), p. 74.
51. Chatterji, R. (ed., 1985): Politics in West Bengal, An Article by Apurba Mukhopadhyay titled *The Left in West Bengal: Government and Movement, 1967-1982,* The World Press Pvt. Ltd., p. 98.

52. Sangothito Chhatra Andolaner Panchas Bacharer Aitijya O Uttaradhikar, published by SFI, West Bengal State Committee, 1971, p. 68 & www.sfiwb.org

53. Acharya, A. (ed., 1998 & 2014), Shat-Sattarer Chhatra Andolan, An Article by Asim Chatterjee, published by Anustup, Kolkata, and enlarged edition, p. 21.

7

Impact of the Movement on Contemporary Society and Economy

The movement launched by the students had left a deep impact in a number of ways. The patriotism, sacrifice and courage of the students earned great respect from the common people. Their movements have strengthened the forces of modernization as they stand for radical reorganization of society. In West Bengal, the popular protest movements including students have upheld the cause of the sharecroppers so that they may get a reasonable share of the produce. Even these movements led to accelerate the process of land reforms, liquidation of rural indebtedness, distribution of surplus land among the rural poor, eviction of jotedari system and finally Operation Barga. On the other hand, influence of the student movements have been perhaps most pronounced in the literary and cultural life of the state. In literature, writers and poets like Manik Bandyopadhyay, Mahasweta Devi, Samaresh Majumder, Subhash Mukhopadhyay, Dinesh Das, Manindra Roy have introduced a new tone and outlook.[1] The radical students habitually recite their poems in the various meetings and demonstrations. In the public meetings, rallies and demonstrations the agitating students staged dramas, which helped to create a new outlook. In addition to these, the students brought out many leaflets, booklets, Chharas or rhymes which also influenced the common masses of Bengal.

SOCIAL IMPACT

The extensive and self-sacrificing participation of the

students in the socio-economic and political issues forms a glorious episode of Indian history in the 20th century. At the same time for over a century, student movement has been one of the India's most serious educational and political problems.[2] Prof. Humayun Kabir analyzed the roots of student indiscipline in India. According to him, the loss of leadership by teachers, growth of economic difficulties, defects in the existing system and general loss of idealism led to the students' dissatisfaction in India. A large number of students are drawn from social strata which cannot provide them with minimum needs.[3]

In Afro-Asian countries, students represent very important and vocal segment of the population. They constitute a significant ratio of the movements in their respective societies. As such they play an important role in the socio-economic and political movements in the country.

IMPACT ON BANGLADESH LANGUAGE MOVEMENT

The Bengal student movement had left a deep impact on the Bangladesh Language Movement and Liberation War. Bangladesh had long experienced student turbulence and its diverse manifestations, over and over again accompanied with police firings. In the Language Movement of Bangladesh, the students and youths played an important role. The excitement of religious nationalism received its first rage when the ruling elites of Pakistan decided to make Urdu as the sole language of Pakistan, consciously ignoring the fact that Urdu speaking Pakistanis did not exceed 3 percent of the total population. The majority in Pakistan which included all Bengali Muslims forming 54 percent of the population did not even understand Urdu language. On September 2, 1947 some students of Dhaka University formed Tamaddum Majlish, a cultural organization. During the first phase of the language movement this organization campaigned vigorously for making Bengali the medium of education and of legal proceedings. On September

15, 1947 they brought out a pamphlet titled "should Pakistan's state language be Urdu or Bengali"? In that pamphlet they demanded Bengali to be the medium of instruction in educational institutions, all legal matters and of all official works and also the language of the Central Government of Pakistan.[4] At this critical juncture, Md. Ali Zinnah and Liaquat Ali Khan were swift to understand the growing spirit of Bengali nationalism. They knew that East Bengal was the seat of Bengali culture and Bengali language. On his first official visit to East Bengal in February, 1948, Zinnah declared that Urdu alone would be the national language of Pakistan. East Bengal reacted sharply. It aggravated a never ending series of protests and resistance movements. The protests were led by a young student leader Sheikh Mujibur Rahaman who was tortured by police and later taken into custody. East Bengal felt that their esteemed culture and way of life were endangered. After the arrest of Sheikh Mujibur Rahaman, the volcano of anger against West Pakistan erupted in 1952 in the form of language riots spearheaded by the students of Dhaka University. A big demonstration brought out against the Government's declaration about Urdu being the state language was held on February 21, 1952. Prohibiting orders were promulgated to crush the agitation but these were defied by the students. This resulted in police firing, killing and injuring a number of students. This day came to be known as 'Saheed Dibas' or Martyr's Day. Faced with the strong protest, Bengali was made a national language together with Urdu in 1954.[5]

IMPACT ON BANGLADESH LIBERATION WAR

The Bangladesh freedom struggle brought its youth and students to the forefront and involved them in a most violent and vicious conflict. They fashioned the majority in such fighting organizations as the Mukti Bahini and Rakhi Bahini as well as other guerilla groups.[6] Students provided much of the man power of mass demonstrations and in some areas they assumed the leadership of the Mukti Movement.

After Independence, Bengal witnessed a series of student unrest, but these movements could not take shape as all India character, except the movements of the sixties. However, their movements have rocked many universities and colleges and surprised State Government while student unrest and indiscipline of various kinds, related mostly to campus oriented issues, occur in every state, some of the states have been affected by major student disturbances concerning broader socio-economic issues[7] and the West Bengal was first class nursing home of them.

IMPACT ON LITERATURE

Impact of the student movement has been most profound in the field of literature. Sukanta Bhattacharyya was hailed as the great poet. He symbolized a new revolutionary culture and was looked upon as a praiseworthy promoter of the tradition of revolt. Another renounced writer Manik Bandyopadhyay wrote a novel titled 'Chinha' (In Bengali) in the light of student movement of Bengal during colonial and post-colonial period. The writer sharply highlighted the activities of the students in the freedom movement. At the same time he also criticized the post-independence student politics like Pandit Nehru and advised that politics must be the course of study for the students.[8] Subhas Mukhopadhyay was the leading poet of West Bengal for several decades. He was associated with the leftist politics, and as such he roamed village to village, mixed with workers and peasants, took shelter in their huts for a night's rest, and used their vocabulary in his poems.[9] Another literary genious in this field was Mahasweta Devi, a noted social worker and creative writer. Agnigarva, Hazar Churashir Maa and Aranyer Adhikar were the three relevant works, wrote in the light of unpopular activities of the then Government and marked protest in her writings. In the preface of her novel Agnigarva reflects the background of the Naxalbari Movement. She pointed out that "The main cause of the grief of this area is the land owned by the tea gardeners. Here, almost all the labourers are brought by the tea gardeners from outside. These outsiders have become local settlers with the passage of time. They have always faced disaster due to severe exploitation. The tea gardeners here had surplus land and they distributed it among the labourers fully loyal to them. The Government witnessing this transaction deliberated over the question of taking over this surplus land, but the plan of doing this was later for shaken which generated disaffection in the community of the labourers. In the mid 50s in these tea gardens 'adhiers' began agitating against the tea gardeners. Mainly the demand was bringing the surplus land of the tea garden owners within the Government control and thereafter the distribution of this surplus land among them. This agitation became vehemently violent after 1959. Consequently, tea gardeners drove out the adhiers from the tea gardens, demolished their hutment with the elephants. The result was that the peasants of Naxalbari took up arms against this and protested in an organized manner. Later this rebellion provided inspiration to the deprived and exploited peasants of Andhra Pradesh, Kerala, Tamil Nadu, Bihar and Orissa."[10]

Novelists like Nabendu Ghosh, Narayan Ganguly, Gunamoy Manna, Gopal Haldar, Samaresh Majumdar, Samaresh Basu, Sabitri Roy belongs to the popular movements of Bengal and their protests reflected in their writings. Their works hardly ever failed to focus the struggles of the common people, their joys and sufferings, and their noble sentiments.[11]

IMPACT ON SUBALTERN WOMEN

The subaltern women of Bengal were, to some extent, inspired by the movements of the students in the 1960s and

1970s. They came out from pardah and inspired to participate in various popular protests movements. If we carefully study the different protests and popular movements, we found that a sizeable number of subaltern women participated in those movements and in some cases they were forefront in the movement. The living example was the Naxalbari Peasant Movement, where the subaltern women were forefront and even eight subaltern women were shot dead out of 11 people by the police firings.[12]

ECONOMIC IMPACT

The socio-economic protest movements of Bengal and the student participation in it soon spread over other states of India. A wind of change, however, began to blow in some other states. In Gujrat and Bihar strong student and youth movements sprang up against rising prices, food shortage, high unemployment and government corruption. To this was added the prolonged railway men's strike in May, 1974. The communists, however, failed to take any active role in these movements. The democratic movement launched under the leadership of Jayprakash Narayan spread rapidly in a large part of the country.[13]

After Independence, West Bengal inherited a very complicated agrarian structure, where the landlords at the top, intermediaries or Zamindars and jotedars in the middle, and Peasants and Bargadars at the lowest level. The peasants and bargadars cultivated a considerable portion of the land that belonged to the zamindars and jotedars. They did not have legal protections that secure their tenure or terms of eviction. It created unequal access to the social and political power. In these perspective, the land reforms began with the passage of three Acts—The West Bengal Bargadar Act (1950), The West Bengal Estate Acquisition Act (1952), and The West Bengal Land Reforms Act (1955). These three Acts were passed by the

Congress Government of the state. But the legal provisions were not seriously enforced. The primary objective of land reforms has been to bring about an equitable distribution of land in the rural society and to correct the skewed pattern of land tenure system so that the intermediary interests on land are eliminated and security of tenure of the actual tiller of the soil is ensured. Necessary legislative measures have been taken for elimination of intermediary interests imposition of ceiling on holdings, distribution of surplus land to the landless and near landless, safeguarding the rights of the sharecroppers, prevention of alienation of tribal land and continuous updating of land records.[14] By legislative measures the ceiling of the land holding has been changed from individual to family and the term 'land' has been redefined to bring all categories of land under the ceiling.

One who cultivates land owned by somebody else on condition of delivering a share of the produce is a sharecropper, also known as Adhiar, Kisani Bhagidar or Bargadar in the different areas of the state. Their interest in land was not given any protective coverage under any law and they were at the mercy of the land owners till 1950 when a legal provision was made to safeguard their interests in cultivating, possessing and also securing their share of the produce. Ultimately, the West Bengal Land Reforms Act, 1955, made their cultivating right fully protected and heritable so as to ensure their total involvement in the land under their possession which is a pre-condition for optimum utilization of the land. Even then eviction could not be stopped because of non-recording of sustainable number of sharecroppers till 1977. The ascendancy of the Left Front Government to power in 1977 marked the beginning of the massive land reforms programmes. To motivate such sharecroppers to come forward and approach the revenue authorities for recording their names in the RoR a unique method was adopted by the State Government by holding evening meetings in the villages, where bargadars came to convince them of the great advantages of such recording and of their rights and also their obligations. People from the Panchyats and the Peasants' Organizations were involved in such meetings. This path-breaking scheme launched in 1978 is known as Operation Barga. Under the scheme the bargadar is not required to go to the revenue officials, instead the revenue officials themselves have to remain present in the villages to receive the applications, enquire on the spot and publish a list of eligible sharecroppers after necessary hearing of the witnesses and the land owners then and there. By recording their status, bargadar or sharecroppers were finally able to avail themselves of the protections of the LRA without fear of eviction.[15] No new legislation was passed. Rather this programme sought to record names as originally provided for, but never actually done, under the LRA. Operation Barga appears to be the zenith of all the anti-feudal struggles of the past, the programme itself was a struggle, which received state support. This method paved the way for successfully recording the names of the several lakhs of sharecroppers.[16] This has been highly appreciated by scholars and social workers working in the rural areas throughout the country and abroad.

NOTES AND REFERENCES

1. Ray, S. (2007): Marxist Parties of West Bengal: 1947-2001, Progressive, Kolkata, pp. 253-255.
2. The UGC Report on the Problem of Student Indiscipline in Indian Universities, 1960.
3. Kabir, H.: Education in New India, Harper & Brothers, New York, 1957, p. 162 and also see Sen Khagendranath: Education and the Nation; An Indian Perspective, Calcutta University Press, 1970, pp. 775-778.
4. Umar, B.(1997): Language Movement, Published in Sirajul Islam (ed): History of Bangladesh (1704-1971), Vol-I, Political History, Asiatic Society of Bangladesh, Dhaka, 1997, p. 438 and

also see Debjani Ghosal's Article on *Birth of Bangladesh and India's Role in the Liberation Struggle of Bangladesh*, published in The Quarterly Review of Historical Studies, Vol. LIV, No- 3&4, October, 2014- March, 2015, Kolkata, pp. 136-137.

5. Ghosal, D.: *Birth of Bangladesh and India's Role in the Liberation Struggle of Bangladesh*, Published in The Quarterly Review of Historical Studies, Vol. LIV, No- 3&4, October, 2014–March, 2015, Kolkata, pp. 136-137.
6. Unpublished Ph.D. Thesis on Student movements in Global Perspective, JNU, found at www.shodhganga.inflibnet.ac.in, pp. 26-27.
7. Ibid, p. 31.
8. Bandyopadhyay, M.(2016): *Chinha* (Bengali Novel), found in Manik Bandyopadhyay Rachana Samagra, Vol-5, Paschim Banga Bangla Academi, Kolkata, Third Reprint, 2016, p. 357.
9. Ray, S. (2007), p. 255.
10. Devi, M. (1978): Agnigarva (Bengali Novel), Karuna Prakashani, Kolkata.
11. Ray, S.(2007), p. 255.
12. Pain, S. K. (2007) : Women in the Naxalbari Uprising: A Historical Overview, Published in the Journal of Indian History, Vol. LXXV/Parts-1-3, April, August, December, 2007, Kerala University, pp. 275-284.
13. Mukhopadhyay, A. (1985): The Left in West Bengal: Government and Movement, 167-1982, published in Politics in West Bengal edited by Rakhahari Chatterji, The World Press Pvt. Ltd., Kolkata, pp. 98-99.
14. West Bengal: 25 Years of Stability and Progress, Published by Government of West Bengal, Kolkata, 2002, pp. 263-264.
15. Bagchi, A. K. (1998): Studies on the Economy of West Bengal since Independence, Economic and Political Weekly, November 21-December 4, 1998.
16. West Bengal: 25 Years of Stability and Progress, published by Government of West Bengal, Kolkata, 2002, pp. 265-266.

8

Findings, Conclusions and Recommendations

FINDINGS

The major findings of the study have been mentioned below:

- The student movement was not only the harvest of Modern Age, but also has clear evidence which took place during the ancient and medieval period as an ongoing process of student agitation according to the time and development of the civilization. But, their character had been changed from time to time.
- In Bengal within India, the first education system with European idealism was initiated and it was very interesting that the Indian student movement was also initiated in Bengal. The youth minds were easily attracted by the European knowledge and wisdom and by the arguments with scientific analysis.
- In post-independence period planned exclusion of Bengal from the benefits of nation building process, rapid decline of its glorious city, influx of millions of refugees, unemployment and growing economic gloom of the people have caused a sense of deprivation among the Bengalee people as also the students. That is why the student movement which lay emphasis on the politics of protest enjoys a large following and support base in the state.

- In the first part of the students' movement, special emphasis was given to the constructive and cultural activities. Gradually the movement was influenced by political issues. And in the last part, the movements were influenced by the Marxist, to some extent Fascist and other political parties at large. As a result of that, the students' organizations became scattered into different wings.
- The goals of the different movements of the students, fighting in different political banners are not only political, but also social, economic, humanistic and cultural.
- The character of the movements of the students of West Bengal began changing since 1960s. Starting as nationalists they gradually assumed left and extreme ideology. In the place of the mass student organizations, a number of local groups mostly of an informal nature have developed.
- The movement of the students of West Bengal at different times has been concerned with issues altering from educational problems to socio-economic issues. Though students often take up issues touching only their own narrow interests, sometimes they also take up causes which do not directly affect them.
- In the period of this study, it was found that most of the student movement had taken place against the unpopular activities of the Independent Government, but in favour of socio-economic development of the country.
- Immediately, after independence, the Congress Party proclaimed that the students should not mingled with politics, students should plunged themselves into studies for the development of the country. But, interestingly, they produced Chhatra Parisad as their students' wing in Bengal only. The other political parties failed to get on with the opinion of the Congress Party.

- The students did not participate in the socio-economic movements all of a sudden. They were to some extent stimulated by the movements of the 1960s of the USA, England, France, Germany, Italy, China, Russia and Afro-Asian countries. In addition to that the students also came to know about the facts of suffered and poverty-stricken people of the Third World which intensified the momentum of this movement.
- From 1947 to 1971, the innumerable number of homeless or refugee people came, the streets, the slums were filled up. At the same time many new colonies were forcibly established, where the large number of refugees including their sons and daughter took shelter. These refugee students have strongly protested and participated against the unpopular activities of the Government. In order to justify my contention, we can cite example for students' agitation of the 1960 onwards. It appears from the profile of leadership of the agitation that most of the student leader either East Bengalis or refugees.
- Another peculiar characteristics of the student participation was that the students of mofussil area either reluctant or non-interested. During the period, Bengal mofussil students were not prepared to expedite their solidarity on the issues.
- The Food Movement of 1959 & 1966 rocked the whole world. In this movement the active role of the students became obvious. It was found that during the Food Movement of 1966 among the 50 martyrs 28 were the students. It means students were always forefront in the movement.
- Another important changing characteristics of the food movement, which we found that after the death of Nurul Islam, the first student martyr of the Food Movement of 1966, the movement spread from Southern part of Bengal

to the Northern part of Bengal especially North Bengal University and its adjoining Siliguri and Naxalbari.

- In the first part of the 1970s it became clear that the intensity of the student movement was dying down. The pioneers including the numberless youth and students began working for bringing a radical change in the political system of the country in the second half of the 1960s. The failure in the organization of the revolutionary programme frustrated these pioneers. For this the radical students and youth beat a tragic retreat.
- After Bangladesh Liberation War, a vacuum in the political scene of West Bengal became conspicuous because of the backing out of the radical students from the path of democratic movement. The said vacuum was inevitably filled up by the SFI and Chhatra Parishad. This makes it clear that the terrorist activities of the radical students could not get any favourable support from the society. It was a tactical failure. Not only in India, but also in America and Europe the high waves of the radical students' movement were gradually receding back to non-entity.
- Their idea about the problems of the peasants and the armed struggle for removing them was not clear. So, the leftist movement deviated from the Naxalbari path of action and degenerated terroristic aggression of the CPI(M-L).
- The Naxalbari and its afterwards student movements partially brought the issue of disputed land settlements on the eyes of everyone and it accelerated the process of re-distribution of land i.e. Operation Barga.
- In the literally and cultural field the student movement had left a deep impact both constructive and destructive.
- The last and vivid finding is that before independence and even post-independence period up to 1970s the students were more attentive to the socio-economic issues and

problems than their own educational issues, but gradually the students and their wings confine their attention mostly in educational institutions for their own narrow interest.

CONCLUSIONS

In the context of the foregoing study and research on the participation of the students in the socio-economic movements of West Bengal, it may be summed up that it was a child of history like all socio, economic and political movements. It set a new trend in the popular movements of West Bengal. The student movements kindled the fire of a new consciousness among the Indian masses. But, they became a poor victim of the politics of manipulation resorted by the various political parties.

The student movements of Post-Independence period up to 1977 definitely slammed against the political monolith of India and in particular West Bengal. A broad survey of the whole range of activities of the various Students' Organization, it comes into belief that the causes leading to the student movements in all flash points of the then Bengal were starkly different from one another.

In the 1960s and 1970s, it was seen that the intensity of the student movement was dying down. The pioneers including the numberless youth and students began working for bringing a radical change in the country. It is clear that a romantic conception about extremist movement pushed the students to terrorism. This entailed their failure in changing to socialism in words and in deeds. If any one looks back to the history of terrorism of the last 400 years, it becomes evident that terrorism does not possess the reasonable analysis of the evolution of society and substitute competent social system. For this the radical students and youths beat a tragic retreat.

If it comes to the discussion about any Peoples'

Organization or Popular Movements, it is assumed that the organization is like a great tree which has its branches, leafs, flowers and fruits giving us to understand and that taking all these it is a complete whole. Shorn of any of these paraphernalia a tree dies and like arises with the loss of any of its wing a peoples' organization or popular movements also faces abolition. Student constitutes an essential branch of the society. This is the reason why component students take interest in different socio-economic issues. These issues make them take recourse to this or that iconoclastic myth adventures. Sometimes they succeed, some time they succumb to discomfiture.

It is not the intention to keep the students, symbolically speaking, confined in an ivory tower far above the currents and cross-currents of the stream of life flowing down below, though that was the nature of life prescribed for the pupil in ancient India. Study was then likened to a tapasya seeking for complete dedication to intellectual and spiritual pursuits. That is not feasible, nor perhaps desirable, under modern circumstances in India. In fact, the modern trends of education depends less on intuition and more on experience. As a future citizen of a socialist-democratic country, the young Indian should have to be keen students of India's socio-economic thinking and try to understand and interpret the incidents that are taking place around him—not in his own country only, but in other domain as well.

RECOMMENDATIONS

After detailed study, field survey, data-analysis, consulting contemporary historical documents and taking personal interviews of the then student leaders, the following recommendations can be done:

- Without having any political ideology the students fought heroically against imperialism in colonial period. Keeping mind of these, it can be recommended that every students' organization should have an independent entity. They should not be influenced by political issues only.

- As a larger and strong part of the society, the students should not confine their attention in the educational institutions for their own narrow interest only; they must involve themselves in removing socio-economic problems of the society for the greater interest of the nation building process.
- After 1960s, we got some instances of extremist student movement, which was destructive in nature. Even the Vice-Chancellor and Principal could not get relief from the hands of extremist agitators. Some scholar students took part in such kind of movements. Later they realize their blunder. In view of that the student should not be involved in destructive movement in the educational institutions.
- During this study and research, it was observed that the youth minds were easily attracted by the European knowledge and wisdom and by the arguments with scientific analysis. So, it will be fruitful if the students can judge the socio-economic-political issues and problems with scientific approach.
- Throughout the whole study and research, it was observed that the students were to some extent influenced by the Indian intelligentsia since the inception of their movements. The legendary example was Derozio and its Young Bengal Movements. At present scenario, the student movements have been deviated from the colonial and post-colonial phase. Here, the intelligentsia can play a vital role by giving positive advice for the reconstruction of student movements in right way.

Appendices

APPENDIX-1

During Indo-Chinese war posters began to show up in different Colleges and Universities of West Bengal containing such rhymes:

"যখনি প্রশ্ন ওঠে যুদ্ধ না শান্তি
আমাদের বেছে নিতে হয় নাকো ভ্রান্তি
আমরা জবাব দিই, শান্তি শান্তি।" (In Bengali)

"Whenever question arises-peace or strife?
Our reply, we want peace, peace and peace"

(English Translation)

"হরেকৃষ্ণ কোঁয়ার
লাল ঘোড়েকা সওয়ার
বঙ্গদেশে রঙ্গ কেন
খোলা চীনের খোঁয়াড়।" (In Bengali)

"Harekrishna Konar
Rider of Red Horse
Why do this drama in Bengal
The Chinese Farm is opened"

(English Translation)

"রণদিভে, রণদিভে
আর কত হে রণ দিবে।" (In Bengali)

"Ranadive, Ranadive
How many wars will follow?"
(English Translation)

During the time of Indo-Pak War the students began pamphleting like this:

"যখনি জনতা চায় চাকরি ও খাদ্য
সীমান্তে বেজে ওঠে যুদ্ধের বাদ্য।" (In Bengali)

"Whenever people want job and food
In the frontier the bugle begins to hoot"
(English Translation)

During the time of Second Left Front Government, the Pro-Naxalite students began pamphleting like this:

"সাম্রাজ্যবাদের দুটি ফ্রন্ট
কংগ্রেস আর যুক্তফ্রন্ট।" (In Bengali)

"Imperialism has two fronts
Congress and United Front"
(English Translation)

"ভোট ভোট করে যারা
সাম্রাজ্যবাদের দালাল তারা।" (In Bengali)

"Those who want vote.....
They are the broker of imperialism."
(English Translation)

(Collected from *Rajnaitik Poto Bhumite Bharatiya Upamahadesher Chhatra Andolan* by Hiren Dasgupta and Harinarayan Adhikary, 1993)

APPENDIX-2

24th May,1967 at Barajharujota (P.S. Naxalbari) minutes before Inspector Sonam Wangdi was killed by an arrow shot by the miscreants. All the police officers were unarmed (as seen in above pictures).

(Collected from 'Maoist Spring Thunder: The Naxalite Movement (1967-1972)' by A. P. Mukherjee, K.P. Bagchi & Company, Kolkata, 2007)

APPENDIX-3

খাদ্য আন্দোলন ১৯৫৯

খাদ্যের দাবি

প্রত্যুত্তর

(Collected from *'Sat-Sattur: Chhatra Andolan'* (In Bengali) by S. Chakraborty, National Book Agency, Kolkata, 2011)

APPENDIX-4

ভাড়া বৃদ্ধি বিরোধী আন্দোলন ১৯৬৫

না চৌধুরী

আজ হরতাল আজ চাকা বন্ধ, ৫ আগস্ট ১৯৬৫

সোনা চৌধুরী

কলকাতা বিশ্ববিদ্যালয়ের সামনে পুলিশের কাঁদানে গ্যাস

(Collected from *'Sat-Sattur: Chhatra Andolan'* (In Bengali) by S. Chakraborty, National Book Agency, Kolkata, 2011)

APPENDIX-5

ধর্মতলার ট্রাম গুমটির সামনে ছাত্রদের উপর পুলিশি

দিকে দিকে ওঠে অবাধ্যতার ঢেউ

উত্তর কলকাতার রাধা সিনেমার সামনে বিক্ষুব্ধ ছাত্রসমাজ ছবি : সোনা [illegible]

(Collected from '*Sat-Sattur: Chhatra Andolan*' (In Bengali) by S. Chakraborty, National Book Agency, Kolkata, 2011)

APPENDIX-6

খাদ্য আন্দোলন ১৯৬৬

ছবি : মোনা চৌধুরী এক মুঠো ভাতের জন্য গ্রাম থেকে শহরে

স্বরূপনগরে নুরুল ইসলামের মৃত্যুর পরদিন বনগাঁ রেশনিং অফিসে আছড়ে পড়েছে জনরোষ, ফেব্রুয়ারি ১৯৬৬

ছবি : মোনা চৌধুরী

(Collected from '*Sat-Sattur: Chhatra Andolan*' (In Bengali) by S. Chakraborty, National Book Agency, Kolkata, 2011)

APPENDIX -7

[illegible] ণে **মিছিল মৌন কিন্তু বাঙ্ময়** - ১৩ মার্চ ১৯৬৬। ফটো 'দৈনিক বসুমতী'। এই মৌন মিছিলে অংশ
[illegible] ন সত্যজিৎ রায়, মৃণাল সেন, সৌমিত্র চট্টোপাধ্যায়, শোভা সেন, অনুপ কুমার এবং আরোও অনেক
[illegible] ত্যিক

বিনা বিচারে আটক ছাত্র নেতাদের মুক্তি চাই। কলকাতা বিশ্ববিদ্যালয়ের উপাচার্য বিধুভূষণ মালিকের সামনে বিক্ষুব্ধ ছাত্রদের অবস্থান। ১৯৬৬, এপ্রিল

(Collected from '*Sat-Sattur: Chhatra Andolan*' (In Bengali) by S. Chakraborty, National Book Agency, Kolkata, 2011)

Glossary

Adhiyar : a share cropper who bore most of the cost of cultivation and was entitled to a 50 percent share of the harvest. The sharing was done in the Jotedar's grain collection yard where the harvested crop had to be transported by the adhiyar. The lease was oral and on an annual basis.

Anchal : a group of villages forms an anchal

Ashrama : In ancient period, where the students went to take education

Bargadar : share-cropper

Benami lands : lands held by landlords under fictitious names to evade the land ceiling laws.

Bengalee : People of Bengal

Bhadralok : Section of the Bengali population, who are highly educated according to western standards and its relatively affluent.

Bidhan Sabha : Legislative Assembly, the Lower House of a State Legislature in India. In West Bengal, it means State Legislature.

Bigha : a measure of land that varies from region to region. In Bengal, a standard bigha is one third of an acre.

Dakshya : unmarried girl students of the *ashramas*

Dharna : sit-in-strike

Gherao : act of surrounding a person or group of people in order to force the acceptance of demands.

Goonda : hoodlum

Hartal : strike

Jotedar : the landowner who, instead of cultivating the land himself, leases it out to share-croppers.

Kisan Sabha : Peasants' Association

Lathi : a stick, a club usually ferruled bamboo.

Lok Sabha : the Lower House of the Indian Parliament

Mahila Samiti : Womens' Association

Naxalbari : Naxalbari is a small area of Siliguri Sub-Division of Darjeeling District. In 1967, after the outbreak of an agrarian movement at Naxalbari, the place is well known in the political atlas of India

Thana : a police station or the area under its jurisdiction

Vedas : The great religious text for the Hindus

Zamindar : a land holder, under the Mughals, a revenue collector; with permanent settlement they were recognised as estate owners by the British, so long as they paid the government revenue.

Bibliography

A. PRIMARY SOURCES:

REPORTS AND PROCEEDINGS:

Calcutta Literary Gazette, 1935

District Census Hand Book, 1965

District Statistical Hand Book, 2001, Bureau of Applied Economy and Statistics, Govt. of West Bengal

Letters of Pandit Nehru to the Chief Ministers of States on 28th August, 1954: Ref. Letters on Discipline by H. Kabir, 1958

Home Political (A), National Archives of India

Home Political, Confidential, File No. 395/1924, West Bengal State Archives

The Indian Annual Register, July-December, 1930

The Indian Annual Register, Published by N. N. Mitra, 1938, Kolkata

The Report of the Radhakrishnan Commission, 1949 Government of India

The UGC Report on the Problem of Student Indiscipline in Indian Universities, 1959 & 1960

West Bengal Legislative Assembly Proceedings, 1950-1972

West Bengal Legislative Council Debates, 1950-69

West Bengal: 25 Years of Stability and Progress, Government of West Bengal, Kolkata, 2002

Leaflets and Booklets:

Chhatra Sangramer Dhara (written in Bengali), Banin Roy, RSP Publication

Khadya Sankater Janya Dayee Ke? Biswa Nath Mukhopadhyay,

CPI Publication, Kolkata.

Personal Interviews with:

Bagchi Dilip, Student Leader of 1960s, NBU, Dated. 10.01.2007

Biswas Nathuram, Student Leader of 1960s, Siliguri, Dated. 05.01.2007

Chakraborty Ramanikanta, Freedom Fighter, Kushmundi, Dakshin Dinajpur. Aged: 95 years, Dated.01.04.2009

Chatterjee Kishan, Student Leader of 1960s, NBU, Dated. 22.01.2007

Dasgupta Pulinbehari, Freedom Fighter, Balurghat, Dakshin Dinajpur, Aged: 92 years, Dated. 31.03.2009

Majumdar Khokan, Extremist Peasant Leader, Naxalbari, Dated. 05.01.2007

Sanyal Kanu, Extremist Peasant Leader, Hatighisa, Darjeeling, Aged: 80 years, Dated. 03.01.2007

B. SECONDARY SOURCES:

English Books:

Ahuja, Ram (1997), Social Problems in India, Second Edition, Rawat Publications, Jaipur

Altbach, Philip G. (1968), Student Politics and Higher Education in India, Daedalus

– –, (1966), The Transformation of the Indian Student Movement, Asian Survey

– –, (ed. 1968), Turmoil and Transition: Higher Education and Student Politics in India, Lalvani Publishing House, Delhi

– –, (1970), Student Revolution: A Global Analysis, Lalvani Publishing House, Delhi

Bandyopadhyay, Sekhar (2009), Nationalist Movement in India: A Reader, Oxford University Press

Bandyopadhyay, Sekhar (ed. 2017), Decolonization and the Politics of Transition in South Asia, Orient Black Swan Pvt. Ltd., Kolkata, Reprinted Version

Banerjee, Anirban (1998), Exploring Student Politics, Published by Manasi Banerjee, Burdwan, West Bengal

Banerjee, Sumanta (1980), In the Wake of Naxalbari, Subarnarekha, Kolkata

Banerjee, Surendranath, (1963), A Nation in the Making: Being the Reminiscences of Fifty Years of Public Life, Oxford University Press

Banerjee, Tarasankar, (1985), Various Bengal: Aspects of Modern History, Ratna Prakashan, Calcutta

Barbara and John, Ehrenreich (1969), The Student Uprising at Home and Abroad, First Modern Paperback Edition, USA

Barma, Sukhabilas (2007), Socio-Political Movements in North Bengal: A Sub-Himalayan Tract, New Delhi

Basu, Pradip (2000), Towards Naxalbari (1953-1967), Progressive Publications, Kolkata

Basu, Sajal (1990), Faction, Ideology and Politics in Bengal, Minerva, Calcutta

Basu, Sibaji Pratim & Dasgupta, Geetisha (ed. 2010), Politics in Hunger Regime: Essays in Right to Food in West Bengal, FrontPage, London/Kolkata

Baurah, Apurba (2002), Student Power in North-East India; Understanding of Student Movements, Regency Publications, New Delhi

Bhattacharya, Bhabani, (1980), Socio-Political Currents in Bengal: A Nineteenth Century Perspective, Vikash Publishing House Pvt. Ltd., New Delhi

Bora, S., (1992), Student Revolution in Assam: 1917-1947, Mittal Publications, New Delhi

Chakrabarti, Prafulla K. (1999), The Marginal Men, Naya Udyog Publication, Kolkata

Chand, Tara, (1972), History of the Freedom Movement in India, 4 vols, Publication Division, Government of India

Chatterjee, Joya (1994), Bengal Divided, Hindu Communalism and Partition, 1932-47, Cambridge

Chatterjee, Partha (ed. 1997), State and Politics in India, Oxford University Press

Chatterjee, Partha (ed. 1998), The Present History of West Bengal, Oxford University Press

Chatterji, Rakhahari (ed. 1985), Politics in West Bengal, The World Press, Kolkata

– –, (ed. 2004), Politics in India, The State, Society, Interface. South Asian Publishers, New Delhi

Chattopadhyay, Goutam, (1980), Bengal's Student Community in Freedom Movement, Charuprakash, Calcutta

Cockburn, Alexander and Blackburn, Robin (ed. 1969): Student Power: Problems, Diagnosis, Action, Penguin, England

Cohen, Alan (2015), A Course in Miracles Made Easy; A Guide for Students, Teachers, the Dedicated and the Curious, Hay House, UK

Crouch, C. (1970), The Student Revolt, The Bodley Head Ltd., London, UK

Damas, Marius (1991), Approaching Naxalbari, Radical Impression, Kolkata

Das, Suranjan & Bandyopadhyay, P.K. (2004), Food Movement of 1959: Documenting A Turning Point in the History of West Bengal, K.P. Bagchi & Company, Kolkata

Debnath, Sailen (ed. 2007), Social and Political Tensions in North Bengal Since 1947, N.L. Publishers, Siliguri

Dhar, P. N. (2000), Indira Gandhi: the Emergency, and Indian Democracy, Oxford University Press

Franda, F. Marcus (1971), Political Development and Political Decay in Bengal, Firma K.L. Kolkata

– –, (1971), Radical Politics in West Bengal, Massachusetts Institute of Technology

Galeeson, Patrick (19690, Essays on the Student Movement, Columbus, Merrill

Ghosh, Shibdas (1974), Tasks Ahead of the Students and Youths, Suci Publication, Kolkata

Ghosh, Shyamal Kumar (2014), Naxalite Student-Youth Movement of 1970, Sopan Publisher, Kolkata

Ghosh, S. K., (1969), The Student Challenge Round the World, Eastern Law House Pvt. Ltd., Calcutta

Ghosh, Suniti (2000), The Historic Turning Point: A Liberation Anthology, Vol-I, Kolkata

Gopal, Surendra (1976), Jawaharlal Nehru, A Biography, vol. 1, Oxford University Press

Guha Roy, Siddhartha (2007), Calcutta Tramways: A Study of Working Class History (1920-1967), Progressive Publishers, Kolkata

Hazany, Subhesh, (1987), Student Politics in India, Ashish Publishing House

Hundred Years of University of Calcutta, (1957), Calcutta University Publications

Ibram, H. Rogers (2012), The Black Campus Movements; Black Student and the Racial Reconstitution of Higher Education, 1965-1972, Palgrave Macmillan

Joshi, P. C., (1997), Student Revolts in India: Study of Pre-Independence Student Movement, Bombay

– –, (1966), Social Background of Student Unrest, Mainstream

Kabir, Humayun (1957), Education in New India, Harper & Brothers, New York

Llyer, M.A. Cambridge (2007), The Bloody Millennium Internal Conflict in South Asia, University Press

Majumdar, R. C. (ed. 1961), History of the Freedom Movement in India, Vol. III, Firma K. L., Calcutta

Menon, V. P (2017), The Transfer of Power, Orient Black Swan Pvt. Ltd., Kolkata, Reprinted Version

Mishra, Buddhadeb (2014): Quest and Struggle; Student Movements in India, Blaunske Nirdita

Mitra, Sisir (1980), A Public Facility, Its Management and Workers: A Case Study of the Calcutta Tramways, Its Growth and Decay: 1939-1975, People's Publishing House, New Delhi

Mondal, Monika (2011), Setting the Unsettled, Manohar, New Delhi

Mukherjee, Arun Prosad (2007), Maoist Spring Thunder: The Naxalite Movement (1967-1972), K. P. Bagchi & Company, Kolkata

Nehru, Jawaharlal (Abridged Edition, 1989), The Discovery of India, Oxford University Press

Ojha, Krittibas (2001), Charka- Bullet- Ballot, NBA, Kolkata

Palit, Chittabrata (1980), New Viewpoints on Nineteenth Century Bengal, Progressive Publishers, Kolkata

– –, (1975), Tensions in Bengal Rural Society, Progressive Publishers, Calcutta

Pant, Harsh V. (2016), Indian Foreign Policy, Orient Blackswan Pvt. Ltd., Kolkata

Paul, Bappaditya (2014), The First Naxal, Sage Publication Pvt. Ltd., New Delhi

Raghavan, Srinath (2014), 1971; Global History of the Creation of Bangladesh, Orient Black Swan, New Delhi

Rajmwale, Anil (2001), History of Student Movement in India: Origin and Development (1920-1947), Manak Publication Pvt. Ltd., New Delhi

Ray, Sudhir (2007): Marxist Parties of West Bengal (1947-2001), Progressive Publishers, Kolkata

Ross, Aileen D., (1969), Student Unrest in India, London

Roy, Anil Baran (1977), Students and Politics in India, Manohar, New Delhi

Sahu, D.R. (2013), Sociology of Social Movement, Sage Publication Pvt. Ltd., New Delhi

Samaddar, Ranabir (2013), Passive Revolution in West Bengal, 1977-2000, Sage Publication Pvt. Ltd., New Delhi

Samanta, Amiya Kumar (1984), Left Extremist Movement in West Bengal: An Experiment in Armed Agrarian Struggle (Ph. D. thesis of Calcutta University), Firma KLM Pvt. Ltd., Kolkata

Sengupta, Nitish (2001), History of the Bengali Speaking People, UBS Publishers, Kolkata

Sarkar, S. N. (1974), Student Unrest: A Socio-Psychological Study, Indian Book Exchange, Kolkata

Sarkar, Sumit (1973), The Swadeshi Movement in Bengal, 1903-1908, PPH, Delhi

Sarkar, Sushobhan, (1970), Bengal Renaissance and Other Essays, PPH, Delhi

Seal Anil (1968), The Emergence of Indian Nationalism, Oxford University Press

Sen, Khagendranath (1970), Education and the Nation; An Indian Perspective, Calcutta University Press, Kolkata

Sen, Sunil (1982), Peasant Movement in India: 19th and 20th Centuries, K. P. Bagchi & Company, Kolkata, 1982

Shah, Ghanshyam (2004), Social Movements in India, Sage Publication Pvt. Ltd., New Delhi

Shah, Ghanshyam (ed. 2002), Social Movements and the State, Sage Publication Pvt. Ltd., New Delhi

Syed, Rashid Ali (1997), Culture of Student Politics, Inter India Publications, New Delhi

V. Sankar, Nayer (1985), Swadeshi Movement: The Beginning of Student Unrest in South India, Mittal Publications, New Delhi

Bengali Books:

Acharya, Anil (ed. 2014), Shat-Sattarer Chhatra Andolan, Anustup, Kolkata, 1998 and Enlarged Edition

Basu, Jyoti (1998), Jata Dur Mone Pore, NBA, Kolkata

Basu, Jyoti (1986), Janaganer Sange, National Book Agency, Kolkata

Chakraborty, Dipankar & Khasnobis, Ratan (ed. 1989), Aneek, Panchis Bachhar, Prabandha Sankalan, Murshidabad

Chakraborty, Shyamal (2011), 60-70 Er Chhatra Andolan, Pratham Khanda, National Book Agency, Kolkata

Chattopadhyay, Goutam (1980) Swadhinata Sangrame Banglar Chhatra Samaj, Charuprakash, Kolkata

Das Adhikary, Swapan(ed. 1997), Adhuna Jalarka: Sattarer Sahid Lekhak Shilpi Samkhya, Published by Dilip Chakraborty, Kolkata

Das, Jibesh (1998), Uttar Dinajpur Ziller Itihas, (British O Uttar British Parba), Biswagan, Kolkata

Das, Sukumar (1982), Uttar Banger Itihas, Kumar Sahitya Prakasha, Kolkata

Dasgupta, Hiren and Adhikary, Harinarayan (1993 & 2008), Rajnaitik Poto Bhumite Bharatiya Upamahadesher Chhatra Andolan, School for People, Medinipore, 1993 and Radical Impression, Kolkata, 2008

Dasgupta, Sudangshu (2010), Swadhinata Sangrame Sasastra Biplabider Bhumika, NBA, Kolkata

De, Barun (ed. 2008), Mukti Sangrame Banglar Chhatrasamaj, Paschimbanga Itihas Samsad, Kolkata

Devi, Mahasweta (1981), Sattarer Dashak O Tar Par, Anustup, Kolkata

Dutta, Satyabrata (2002), Banglar Bidhansabhar Eksho Bachhar, Progressive Publishers, Kolkata

Haque, Azizul (1991), Karagare 18 Bachhar, Dey's Publishing, Kolkata

Majumdar, Khokan (2004), Naxalbari: Bharater Booke Basanter Vajranirghos, Published by N. C. Roy, Siliguri

Manna, Mahmudur Rahman (2018), Bangladesher Chhatrarajnitir Otit, Bartaman and Bhabishat, Shikha Prokashoni, Dhaka, Bangladesh

Mitra, Saibal (1990), Sater Chhatra Andolan, Published by Pratap Kumar Roy, Aajkaal Publisher Pvt. Ltd. Kolkata

Mohammad, Hannan (1986), Bangladesher Chhatra Andoloner Itihas: Pratham Khanda (1830-1952), Published by Bimal Sarkar, Granthalok, Dhaka, Bangladesh

Mohammad, Selim (2006), Master Da Surya Sen O Banglar Yuvasamaj, Punasha, Kolkata

Mukherjee, Arijit,(2018), Banglar Chhatra Andoloner Dalil, Nabajatak, Kolkata

Roy, Suprakash (2009), Bharater Jatiyatabadi Baiplobik Sangram, Second Edition, Radical Impression, Kolkata

Sarkar, Jibesh (2004), Darjeeling Ziller Communist Andolan Prosange, CPI (M) Darjeeling District Committee, Siliguri

Sengupta, Swaraj (2006), Siksha: Ek Nisabda Biplob, Renaissance Publishers, Kolkata

C. NEWSPAPERS, PERIODICALS & JOURNALS IN ENGLISH (RELEVANT ISSUES & COPIES)

Economic & Political Weekly

Frontier

Frontline

Journal of Indian History

Liberation

New Age

Peoples' Democracy

Social Scientist

The Quarterly Review of Historical Studies

The Statesman

The Telegraph

The Times of India

D. NEWSPAPERS, PERIODICALS & JOURNALS IN BENGALI (RELEVANT ISSUES & COPIES)

Ananda Bazar Patrika

Aneek

Bartika

Chhatra Sangram

Dakshin Desh

Desh Hitaishi

Deshabrati

Ebong Jalarka

Ganabarta

Ganashakti

Jugantar

Kalantar

Kiratbhumi

Lokmot

Loksebak

Madhuparni

Marxbadi Path

Paschim Dinajpur Sambad Prabaho

Pratidin

Suryapur Barta

Teesta Parer Brityanta

Uttar Banga Sambad

Uttar Prasanga

Uttarasha

E. NEWSPAPERS, PERIODICALS & JOURNALS IN NEPALI (RELEVANT ISSUES & COPIES)

Himalaya Darpan

Himalchuli

Sagarmatha

Sunchari

F. NEWSPAPERS, PERIODICALS & JOURNAL IN HINDI (RELEVANT ISSUES & COPIES)

Dainik Jagaran

Janapath Samachar

Viswamitra

G. NOVEL IN BENGALI

Bandyopadhyay, Manik, Chinha, Manik Rachna Samogra, Vol-V, Paschimbanga Bangla Academy, Kolkata, 1999

Devi, Mahasweta, Agnigarva, Karuna Publisher, Kolkata 1978

Devi, Mahasweta, Hazar Churasheer Maa, Karuna Publisher, Kolkata, 1978

Majumdar, Samaresh, Kalbela, Ananda Publisher, Kolkata, Paila Baisakh, 1390 Bangabda

Majumdar, Samaresh, Uttaradhikar, Mitra & Ghosh Publisher, Kolkata, 1979

Mitra, Ashok, Apila Chapila, Ananda Publishers, Kolkata, 2003

H. AUTOBIOGRAPHIES & MEMOIRS IN BENGALI:

Basu, Jyoti, Jato Dur Mone Pore, NBA, Kolkata, 1998.

– –, Janaganer Sange, Vol-I & II, National Book Agency, Kolkata, 1986 & 1991

Guha, Kamal, Amar Jiban Amar Rajniti, Deep Prakashan, Kolkata, 2002

Jha, Manik, Alor Pathik Comred Manik Jha, CPI(M), Malda District Committee, Malda, 2001

I. INTERNET SOURCES:

http://hep.oise.utoronto.ca/index.php/hep/ar

http://studentmovementsinindia.blogspot.in/2

http:/mail.sarai.net/piper mail/reader-list/2007

http;//www.primopdf.com

https:/aisfhariyana.wordpress.com/about

www.mcrg.ac.in

www.sfiwb.org

www.shodhganga.inflibnet.ac.in

www.ugc.ac.in

J. ORAL HISTORY

Index

A

Academic Association 59, 63
Afro-Asian countries 121
AICCCR 40
AICCR 155
All India College Students Conference (AICSC) 73
Ajijul Haque 150
Ajoy Mukherjee 139, 144
All Bengal Students' Association (ABSA) 74
All Bengal Teachers Association (ABTA) 99, 100
All India College Students Conference (AICSC) 73
All India Students Convention 75
All India Students' Federation (AISF) 75, 85
All-India Muslim Students Federation (AIMSF) 76
Amrita Bazar Patrika 82, 104, 126
Ananda Bazar Patrika 97, 105, 127, 130, 131, 153, 157
Anti Fascist League 119
Anti-Circular Society 67-69
Anti-Merger Movement 88, 102
Anti-partition movement. 66
Ashrama 52
Ashutosh College 38, 96
Asian and African Countries 115
Asim Chatterjee 29, 43, 121, 136, 150
Aurobindo Ghosh 72, 129
Azad Hind Fauj 77

B

Baby boom 111
Backward Caste Movements 31
Bamandas Mandal 99
Bangabasi College Students 153
Bangiya Sahitya Parisad 49, 80
Bangla Congress 139, 144
Bangladesh Liberation War 160
Banglay Bampanthi Chhatra Andolan 103
Bargadar 145
Barricade Movement 93
Bengal National College 70
Bengal Renaissance 64
Bengal Students' Movement 29, 116
Bengal Technical Institute 70
Bengalee 25, 78
Berkeley Revolt 112
Bethune College 74
Bidhan Chandra Roy 97, 101
Bolshevik Revolution 119

BPSA 75
BPSF 91, 93, 100, 159
British Rulers 22
Brotherhood 73

C

Calcutta Medical College 92
Calcutta University 40, 69, 91, 133
Carlyle Circular 68
Charu Chandra College 91
Charu Majumdar 41, 43, 151, 157, 158
Chhatra Andolan 37, 50
Chhatra Bloc 86
Chhatra Parisad 86, 153, 160
Chinese Communist Party 152
Chinese Revolution 116
Civil Disobedience Movement 75
Columbia University 112
Communist Party 31, 85, 130
Communist Party of India (CPI) 93, 94
Communist Party of India (Marxist-Leninist) CPI (M-L) 29, 33, 40, 155, 156, 158, 161
Communist Party of India (Marxist) 143, 144, 151, 153, 155
Congress Party 32, 85

D

Dalit Movements 31
Dawn Society 66, 69
Derjeeling district 40
Derozian movement 30
Derozio 56, 142
Deshhitaishi Sabha 63
Dilip Bagchi 135, 144, 146, 148, 150
Durbhiksha Pratirodh Committee 129
Durgapur High School 159

E

Economic crisis 49, 124, 160
Electoral Politics in West Bengal 31
Employment crisis 84
Extremist movement 42

F

Food and fuel crisis 134
Food crisis 84
Food Movement 28, 34, 36, 45, 125, 134, 135, 136
Ford Foundation Foreign Area Training Program 32
Forward Bloc 86, 94
French Revolution 23, 54, 57, 58

G

Gandhi-Subhash-Rabindranath 158
Gandhiji 73, 88
Global Student Movement 49
Gopal Sen 159

H

Hartal 74
Henry Louis Vivian Derozio 57
Hindu College 23, 57, 58

Hindu Mela 64
Historic Food Movement 124
House of Derozio 58
Hunger strikes 92

I

Ilbert Bill 65
Imperialistic education system 55
Independent Committee on Vietnam' (ICV) 112
Indian Association 65
Indian Freedom Movement 30
Indian National Liberation Movement 28
Indira Gandhi 33, 138
Indo-Chinese 130, 132
Ishwar Tirki 144, 145

J

Jadavpur University 129, 159
Jangal Santal 144, 150
Japanese students movement 116
Jawaharlal Nehru 75, 84
Joint Strike Committee 97
Jotedars 142, 144, 146, 148, 156
Jyoti Basu 94, 100

K

Kanu Sanyal 43, 151, 155
Kisan Chatterjee 121, 135, 144, 145, 146, 147, 148, 150
Krishna Kumar Mitra 69
Krishna Mohan Bandyopadhyay 61
Krishna Mohan Banerjee 59
Krishna Roy 155
Kumkum Bhattacharyya 136,

L

Labourers 60, 147
Lala Lajpat Rai 72, 73
Land Grab Movement 34
Left Movement 40
Leftist movement 161
Leftist student organizations 133
Liberation 40, 41, 75
Liberation Anthology 40, 51
Liberation movement 154
Lok Sevak Sangha 102
London School of Economics (LSE) 113
Lord Curzon 67
Lord Mountbatten 83, 84

M

Mahasweta Devi 39
Majumdar, Ramesh Chandra 81
Mao-Tse-Tung 41, 110, 116,
Martin Luther 88, 118
May Movement 113
Md. Ali Zinnah 75
Middle Class Movements 31
Movement against communal violence 36
Movement of civil liberty 36
Mughal Empire 54
Mujib Regime 90
Muslim League 77

N

Nanda Prasad High School 136
Nanterre University 113
Naokhali riots 90
National Liberation Movement 31
National University 66
Nationalist movements 115
Naval Mutiny 77, 78
Naxalbari 29, 40, 44, 136, 142, 145, 146, 147, 148, 152, 154
Naxalbari Andolan 39
Naxalbari High School 146
Naxalbari Movement 29, 150, 155, 156
Naxalbari path 161
Naxalbari Peasant Movement 30, 34, 40, 41, 49, 142, 152
Naxalbari Peasant Struggle 151, 152
Naxalbari Peasant Uprising 29
Naxalbari to Srikakulam 158
Netaji Subhash Chandra Bose 73
North Bengal University 40, 129, 135, 147
Nurul Islam 135

P

Pabitra Pani Saha 135, 144, 146, 148
Para-military 101, 146
Paris Revolution 119
Peasant and Labour Movements 110
Peasant Association 145
Peasant Movements 31
Peasants' Association 145
Prafulla Chandra Ghosh 73, 155
Prafulla Sen 134
Praja Socialist Party 96
Praja Socialist Party (PSP) 94
Pratirodh Committee 94
Presidency College 40, 43, 74, 136, 147, 150
Press Advisory Council 97
Progressive Students' Union 86
Promod Kumar Ghosal 74
Public Distribution System 125

R

Rabindranath Tagore 66, 72
Radha Binode Pal 97
Radhakrishnan Commission 124
Radical Student 59
Radical Students' Federation 153
Raiganj University College 101
Raja Rammohan Roy 56, 63
Rambola Jote 145
Rammohan Library Hall of Calcutta 151
Red Guard Organization 41
Refugee Movement 28, 36
Refugee People 98
Refugees 46, 79, 93
Rehabilitation 84, 91
Revolutionary 41, 118, 119, 147
Revolutionary Socialist Party (RSP) 86, 94

Riots 133
Ripon College of Calcutta 73
Rudhir Ashrama 52
Russian Revolutionary Movement 115

S

Saibal Mitra 29, 121, 134, 150
Sanskrit College 62
Santiniketan 100
Scottish Church College 153
Siliguri College 40
Simon Commission 73, 74
Sister Nivedita 66
Social movements 44
Socialist Unity Centre of India (SUCI) 94
Socio-Economic Movements 26
Sorbonne University 113
Soviet Society 115
Soviet Union 118
Strasbourg University 113
Student Federation 138
Student Leaders 100
Student Movement of England 113
Student Movement of France 113
Student Movement of Germany 114
Student Movement of Russia 115
Student Movement of Spain 114
Student Participation 26, 71
Student Revolution 110
Students Federation 130, 153
Students' Movements 31
Students' Organization 47
Surendranath Banerjee 65, 69

T

Tarinicharan Banerjee 59, 62
Teachers' movement 28, 36, 88
Tear gas 91, 128
Tebhaga Movement 78
Tejarat Hussain 129
Thomas Paine 23, 54, 57
Toulouse University 113
Trade Union 87
Tram Fare 36, 37, 88, 94
Tram Fare movement 98
Tramways workers 93
Tribal Movements 31

U

Uma Charan Basu 58, 59
Unemployment 31, 85, 160
United Central Refugee Council (UCRC) 34, 92
United Front 31, 32, 34, 40
United Front Government 144, 155, 156
University Grants Commission (UGC) 87

V

Vande Mataram 68
Vietnam Liberation Movement 119
Vietnamese Liberation War 154
Vishwa Yuvak Kendra 27
Visva Bharati University 100, 129

Vidyasagar College 73

W

West Bengal College and University Association 101
Women's Movement 31
Working Class Movements 31

Y

Yankee imperialism 117
Young Bengal 23, 33, 56, 57
Youth Upsurge 33

Z

Zamindars 71, 78